Power
Research Tools

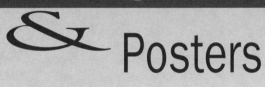

Learning Activities

& Posters

**JOYCE
KASMAN
VALENZA**

ILLUSTRATED BY
EMILY VALENZA

**AMERICAN
LIBRARY
ASSOCIATION**
Chicago
2003

Composition by the dotted i using QuarkXPress 4.1, Macintosh platform. Typefaces: Caxton Book and Univers

The paper used in this publication meets the minimum requirements of American National Standard for Information Sciences—Permanence of Paper for Printed Library Materials, ANSI Z39.48-1992. ⊚

Library of Congress Cataloging-in-Publication Data
Valenza, Joyce Kasman.
    Power research tools : learning activities and posters / Joyce Kasman Valenza
       p.   cm.
    Includes bibliographical references and index.
    ISBN 0-8389-0838-1
    1. Research—Methodology—Study and teaching. 2. Information retrieval—Study and teaching. 3. Internet searching—Study and teaching. 4. Electronic information resource literacy—Study and teaching. 5. Report writing—Study and teaching.
    I. Title.
    ZA3075 .V35 2002
    001.4′2′072—dc21   2002008972

Printed in the United States of America.

07 06 05 04 03   5 4 3 2 1

CONTENTS

POSTERS   *vii*

ACKNOWLEDGMENTS   *ix*

INTRODUCTION   *xi*

1. SEARCHING   *1*

What Is a Thesis?   *6*

From Topic to Thesis: Walking through the Process   *8*

Boolean Aerobics   *11*

"3M" Chart   *12*

Before You Logon: Planning Your Search   *13*

Search Tool Species: A Field Guide   *14*

Practicing Search Strategies   *17*

Focusing a Topic for Research   *18*

Practice Focusing a Topic   *19*

SearchQuest: A WebQuest about Search Tools   *20*

Search Tool Organizer   *21*

The Big Decision: Subject or Keyword Searching   *22*

Visualizing the Search Process   *23*

Power Searching Tips for the Web and Online Databases   *24*

Why a Subject Directory? (High School)   *26*

Why a Subject Directory? (Middle/Intermediate School)   *27*

Web Scavenger Hunt   *28*

Resource Page for Web Scavenger Hunt   *29*

Using Experts as Information Sources   *30*

Search Planner   *32*

2. ETHICS   *33*

Discouraging Plagiarism: Advice for Teachers   *37*

Is It Plagiarism? A Discussion   *38*

Ethics Questionnaire   40

When Should I Document Sources in My Text?   42

Plagiarism versus Documentation   44

Documenting Your Sources   46

Citing Online Sources   48

Works Cited and Works Consulted Pages   51

Source Cards   52

Note Cards   54

Quoting, Paraphrasing, and Summarizing   55

Student Guidelines for Multimedia and Web Page Production   56

Permission Letter Template   58

Weaving Quotes into Your Writing   59

3. EVALUATION

    60

Evaluation: CARRDSS   65

Why Should I Take This Author Seriously?   66

Ask Yourself Questions   68

Thinking about Your Research: Essential Questions to Assure an "A" Project!   69

Research CheckBric   70

Research Project Rubric   72

Multimedia Project/Web Page Evaluation Rubric   73

Web-Based Pathfinder Rubric   76

Position Paper and Thesis Oral Defense Rubrics   79

Thesis Oral Defense Rubric   80

Research Conference Form   81

Checklist for Research   82

Reflecting on the Research Process   84

Comparing Subscription Services and Search Tools (High School)   85

Comparing Subscription Services and Search Tools (Middle School)   86

Practice Ranking Sources (High School)   87

Practice Ranking Sources (Middle School)   88

Web Page Evaluation Worksheet   89

Annotated Works Cited   91

Evaluating Web Sources for Your Research Project   92

A WebQuest about Evaluating Web Pages   93

Organizer for Evaluating Websites WebQuest   94

4. ORGANIZING AND COMMUNICATING

4. ORGANIZING AND COMMUNICATING ... 95

Question Organizer and Sample Questions ... 99

Changing the Questions (Some Sample Responses) ... 100

Developing Essential Questions for a History Project ... 101

Research Task Requirements Checklist ... 102

Final Steps to a Finished Project ... 103

Thesis Project Organizer ... 104

Current Events Template ... 105

Speech Organizer ... 106

Debate Organizer ... 107

Persuasive Documentary Organizer ... 108

Template for Creating a Pathfinder ... 109

Student Self-Evaluation Checklist ... 111

How to Score More Points with Your PowerPoints ... 112

Storyboard for a Multimedia Presentation ... 113

POSTERS

1. Information Technology Ethics
2. Evaluating Web Resources
3. Citing Your Online Sources
4. Thinking about Questions: Beyond "Topical" Research
5. URLs: Clues to Content
6. Choosing a Search Tool
7. Boolean Operators—OR
8. Boolean Operators—NOT
9. Boolean Operators—AND
10. Brainstorming Keywords
11. Case Sensitivity
12. Effective Searching
13. The Free Web Is Not Enough!
14. Phrase Searching
15. Search Engine Essentials
16. Subject Directories
17. What's Not on the Free Web?
18. Wildcards/Truncation/Stemming

ACKNOWLEDGMENTS

Like any good school library program, this project was a collaborative effort. It includes the work of notables in the field of information literacy—Doug Johnson, Joe Barker, and Bernie Dodge. It also includes the work of friends and colleagues with whom I collaborate daily.

At Springfield Township (Pa.) High School, Principal Joe Roy decided that research was important enough to become the focus of a year's teaching. He encouraged our faculty to test many of these tools across the disciplines. This work would not have been possible without the energy and cooperation of the students and faculty at Springfield. Among them is Language Arts coordinator Carol Rohrbach, who understood the direct connection between information literacy and effective reading and writing and helped me develop and test several of the tools included in this resource. Michael Wagman continues to help me invent as he has over the course of several years, and generously offered his gifted students as testers. Jackie Michelson tested and tweaked some of these pages on the middle-school level. Business teacher Sue Fox, at nearby Hatboro-Horsham High School, adopted the information literacy mission and transformed her basic computer course into a semester of information literacy. My dear friends and secretaries, Joan Schumer and Michele Kennedy, supported my efforts energetically and clerically.

Patrick Hogan continues to trust that I know what librarians need, and Dianne Rooney's keen and creative touch gives polished life to my simple pages.

My "boys," Dennis and Matthew, continue to understand that hugs may be almost as good while I am at the computer. And then there's Emily, my daughter and long-time collaborator, who generously offered her whimsy and talents in yet another of Mom's little projects.

INTRODUCTION

As school or public librarians, teachers, or technology coordinators, we share a mission. We want to make sure our students graduate with a set of usable skills. Whether they enter the job market directly or go on to higher education, one thing is certain—information will dominate their lives. And the Internet will be the place they go to access that information.

In my library I see a generation of Internet-confident students. The Web is their turf. They confidently click around in their searches for information, but as I see it, few reflect on the effectiveness of their research, or their ability to use and communicate information. Few learn, or feel motivated, to improve their research. And few teachers have the real confidence necessary to instruct students in effective research strategies.

We are the first generation of teachers and librarians to address the needs of a student population literally drowning in information. Our instructional strategies must shift. Not only should we address the cognitive skills students must apply to successfully locate, analyze, evaluate, and communicate information, but we must also address the habits and dispositions of a generation for whom information is an easy commodity—"no big deal." If students can access *some* information, why should they struggle to get the best-quality information?

Technology has increased our ability to access information, but much work is yet to be done. We now need to design projects that challenge students to sort through and select the best information, projects that challenge students to go beyond retelling to using information effectively, projects that allow students to practice habits of scholarship. And we need to value and assess the complicated process in which students engage when they research. That process should be practiced and evaluated with regularity. Students need practice in such skills as how to choose the right search tool, how to determine when the *free* Web just won't cut it, how to formulate strategies that will bring the best stuff to the top of a results list, and perhaps most important, how to *use* the information they collect in original, creative, ethical, and effective ways. These information skills, behaviors, and attitudes will serve them and be valued at the university as well as in the world of work.

Power Research Tools offers a guide to the skills and habits students need to become successful adult information seekers and users. This package is both a learning and a teaching tool. Use it to catch up with those skills you may have missed. Use it with other teachers and librarians as a training tool. Use it directly with students as a curriculum, or use only the pieces you need to review targeted skills.

The skills described here correlate to the AASL's (American Association of School Librarians') *Information Power: The Nine Information Literacy Standards for Student Learning* (http://www.ala.org/aasl/ip_nine.html), ISTE's (International Society for Technology in Education's) NETS Project *(National Educational Technology Standards for Students)* (http://cnets.iste.org/), and ACRL's (Association of College and Research Libraries') *Information Literacy Competency Standards for Higher Education* (http://www.ala.org/acrl/guides/ index.html).

These activities and accompanying posters are a curriculum resource for librarians, teachers, tech coordinators, and trainers to help students (and classroom teachers) better navigate new information landscapes.

The book guides teachers in designing more meaningful research activities. It features activities to illustrate the various search tool options and strategies. It includes generic "scaffolding" to guide students through the research process—tools designed to help students develop questions worthy of research, organize the information they collect, evaluate the progress of their research, prepare to communicate new knowledge, and discover their own voices as writers.

The posters reinforce skills introduced in the activities and handouts. Rotate them as you introduce new skills.

As a follow-up to *Power Tools,* which offered the practical tools a school librarian needed to manage a program, *Power Research Tools* offers a similar array of practical tools focused on developing the skills of the student researcher.

Searching

From *Information Power*

Information Literacy

Standard 1: The student who is information literate accesses information efficiently and effectively.

Indicators

1. Recognizes the need for information
2. Recognizes that accurate and comprehensive information is the basis for intelligent decision making
3. Formulates questions based on information needs
4. Identifies a variety of potential sources of information
5. Develops and uses successful strategies for locating information

From *NETS for Students*

5. Technology research tools

Students use technology to locate, evaluate, and collect information from a variety of sources.

From *Information Literacy Competency Standards for Higher Education* (Association of College and Research Libraries)

Standard 1: The information literate student determines the nature and extent of the information needed.

Performance Indicators

1. The information literate student defines and articulates the need for information.
2. The information literate student identifies a variety of types and formats of potential sources for information.
4. The information literate student reevaluates the nature and extent of the information need.

Standard 2: The information literate student accesses needed information effectively and efficiently.

Performance Indicators

1. The information literate student selects the most appropriate investigative methods or information retrieval systems for accessing the needed information.
2. The information literate student constructs and implements effectively designed search strategies.
3. The information literate student retrieves information online or in person using variety of methods.
4. The information literate student refines the search strategy if necessary.
5. The information literate student extracts, records, and manages the information and its sources.

Standard 3: The information literate student evaluates information and its sources critically and incorporates selected information into his or her knowledge base and value system.

Performance Indicator

7. The information literate student determines whether the initial query should be revised.

RELATED POSTERS

Brainstorming Keywords

Boolean Operators—AND

Boolean Operators—NOT

Boolean Operators—OR

Phrase Searching

Case Sensitivity

Wildcards/Truncation/Stemming

Search Engine Essentials

Subject Directories

Choosing a Search Tool

The Free Web Is Not Enough!

Effective Searching

In the electronic information landscape, everyone is a searcher. But our students may feel falsely confident about their ability to search. Effective searching involves far more thought and effort than relying on one favorite search tool and entering the first few words that come to mind. The searching landscape is dynamic and may look completely different every few months. Students need to make choices, identifying and selecting from a selection of search tools—subject directories, search engines, meta-search engines, tools for the "invisible Web," and a growing number of up-and-coming hybrid and smart tools. Different information needs require different searching strategies. Effective searchers take time to think about their searches; they effectively brainstorm keywords and subject headings, understand what they are looking for, and continually mine their results lists for words and strategies to help them further refine their searches.

Not everyone thinks, or needs to think, like a librarian, and we might contribute to information overload and frustration by making searching too complicated a process. It's a tough balance. Although it is a good idea to introduce Boolean strategies, it is most important that students approach the research process thoughtfully, learn to refine their searches, and grasp just a few important searching concepts:

- Choice of words and phrases will dramatically impact the effectiveness of a search.
- AND (+) ensures that all entered terms appear in a results list. (Google works so well for students because it assumes the AND.)
- Phrases (names and titles) may be isolated by quotation marks.
- Except for proper names, search terms should be typed in lowercase letters.
- Choice of search tool is very meaningful. Sometimes you need a subscription database, sometimes you need a search engine, sometimes you need a smarter search engine, and sometimes you need a directory.
- Not everything is on the Web. Books still have great depth and value, and the Web has some very deep holes!

ACTIVITIES AND HANDOUTS

What Is a Thesis? and *From Topic to Thesis:* "Topical research" has limited value in an information-rich landscape. Students need to *use* information to persuade, analyze, compare, and make judgments. Student work should be driven by inquiry and purpose. Topical research inspires little more than printing, and students deserve more worthy challenges. *What Is a Thesis?* (see p. 6) offers a definition of a thesis and advice for developing one. *From Topic to Thesis* (see p. 8) walks students through the process using their own initial topic choices. The activity first models the process with a sample topic. Students then work through a process page in the computer lab. After they complete their own brainstorming, ask them to change seats in the lab and add comments to a classmate's brainstorming.

Boolean Aerobics: Use this activity (see p. 11) to explicitly demonstrate how the AND, OR, and NOT operators are used to broaden or narrow a search. You may have to adapt the criteria for various demographics or for schools requiring uniforms.

"3M" Chart: This chart, developed by Bernie Dodge, professor of educational technology at San Diego State University, focuses students on brainstorming keywords and phrases, and on planning their searches. The chart (see p. 12) can be used as an assessment tool to ensure students reflect on searching syntax before going online. Consider assigning it as homework just before beginning research with a class.

Before You Logon: Planning Your Search: This activity (see p. 13) will ensure students consider their keywords and strategies before logging on and will enable you to assess their understanding of search strategies. Students may use the organizer to record additional keywords they discover, or "mine," during the search process. Assign this as a homework project the day before a visit to the library or lab.

Search Tool Species: A Field Guide: Students have a wide range of searching options. This handout (see p. 14) helps students to narrow the field by understanding the various search tool species.

Practicing Search Strategies: This activity (see p. 17) should demonstrate to students that search strategies *do* make a difference and that each search engine has its own quirky syntax. Don't look for complex strategies here. Be satisfied if students recognize phrases in quotation marks, identify critical words to be "ANDed," consider words that should be excluded, and recognize helpful synonyms.

Focusing a Topic for Research: Moving from topic to keywords to questions to thesis is not an easy process. This activity (see p. 18) focuses on the beginning of the research process and allows students an opportunity to confer with the teacher or librarian after preliminary searching and reading. It is likely the adult will see additional strategies or search tools to help the student improve his or her search.

Practice Focusing a Topic: Use these three topic ideas (see p. 19) to brainstorm keywords and potential questions to explore before turning students loose on their authentic searches.

SearchQuest: This WebQuest (see p. 20) introduces students to a variety of search tools, forcing them to examine each tool's features and specific syntax requirements. The activity should result in students dramatically increasing their searching toolkits. Included here are reproducibles necessary to implement the full unit, posted on the Web at http://mciu.org/~spjvweb/sqstu.html.

Search Tool Organizer: Students should use this tool (p. 21) to guide them through careful exploration of their assigned search tool and to help them prepare their commercials.

The Big Decision: Subject or Keyword Searching: This activity (see p. 22) asks students to identify important words and concepts in particular search examples and to decide whether they are best searched through a keyword or topic search/search engine or subject directory approach.

Visualizing the Search Process: This model (see p. 23) illustrates the recursive process employed by good searchers—reconsidering, refining, and responding at each step.

Power Searching Tips for the Web and Online Databases: This "cheat sheet" (see p. 24) describes most of the common strategies used by search engines and databases. Use this as a handout for more advanced students, emphasizing the unique syntax of each search tool. Though you cannot teach every interface, it helps to understand these broad concepts. Knowing that these strategies exist, and discovering how they are expressed in students' favorite search tools, will significantly improve their searches.

Why a Subject Directory? (High School and Middle/Intermediate School): This comparative activity (see pp. 26 and 27) asks students to test subject directories against search engines for a few commonly researched topics. (It would be best to substitute your own relevant topics here.) The activity usually convinces students that subject directories have value they've never realized.

Web Scavenger Hunt and *Resource Page:* Scavenger hunts work best as tools to introduce the resources students will be using in a specific upcoming project or course. Substitute the resources you want your own students to know about. This activity works best when students approach it as a team. For shorter time frames or for individual work, cut the number of questions. For convenience, post both the hunt (see p. 28) and the resource page (see p. 29) as online documents.

Here are a few answers that might be handy if you choose to use this one "as is":

2. Total distance: 3,187.4 miles (5,129.5 km)
   Total estimated time: 53 hours, 28 minutes

3. Michael Jackson, born 8/29/58, is the oldest
   Michael Jordan, born 2/17/63
   Michael J. Fox, born 6/9/61

18. Web documents generally do not have fixed page numbers or any kind of section numbering. If your source lacks numbering, you have to omit numbers from your parenthetical references.

Using a search tool, students should be able to locate the address for the U.S. Senate and for their own local newspaper.

Using Experts as Information Sources: Students can go beyond search robots to find information. The Web offers students unprecedented access to experts. Some generously offer their services on gateway expert pages. Others may be contacted politely if discovered through their own web pages or through electronic mailing lists and usenet groups. This handout (see p. 30) suggests where and how to contact experts for information.

Search Planner: Ask students to keep this form (see p. 32) in their notebooks as an organizer as well as an in-process assessment tool for any major research project.

WHAT IS A THESIS?

A good thesis statement makes the difference between a thoughtful research project and a simple "regurgitation of facts." A thesis statement declares what you believe and what you intend to prove. A good thesis will help you focus your search for information. It will drive your writing. Each point you make in your project should support your thesis.

Don't rush! You must do a lot of background reading before you know enough about a subject to identify a key or essential question, even more before you can take a stand. You will likely begin your research with a "working" or preliminary thesis that you will continue to refine until you are certain of where the evidence leads.

The thesis statement is typically located at the end of your opening paragraph.

What are the attributes of a good thesis?

- It proposes an arguable point with which people could reasonably disagree. A strong thesis takes a stand. A strong thesis justifies the discussion you will present.
- It tackles a subject that can be adequately covered in the format of the project assigned. It is not too broad or too narrow.
- It is specific, focused. A strong thesis proves a point without discussing "everything about. . . ."
- It avoids general or sweeping statements.
- It clearly asserts your own conclusion based on evidence.
- It should pass the "so what?" or "who cares?" test. This is a scholarly activity. Your thesis should do more than restate the obvious.

How do you move from research to a thesis?

As you read and think about a topic, look for:

- Interesting contrasts or comparisons
- Relationships that are not apparent
- Strong arguments for or against an idea

Consider the following questions:

- Is there something about the topic that surprises you?
- Do you encounter ideas that make you wonder why?
- Does something an "expert" says make you respond, "No way! That can't be right!" or "Yes, absolutely. I agree!"?

Here is an example of developing a thesis

- Select a topic—for instance, television violence and children.
- Ask an interesting question: What are the effects of television violence on children?
- Read through the research, revising as you learn, until you are able to determine a preliminary argument and take a focused stance—for instance, violence in television cartoons increases aggressive behavior in preschool children.

- Remember, this argument is your "preliminary," or "working," thesis. As you read you may discover evidence that may change your stance. It is okay to revise your thesis!

Create a list of questions to guide your research

For example:

- How many hours of cartoons does the average young child watch per week?
- How do we identify a "violent" cartoon?
- How do we define "aggressive behavior" in children?
- Which types of cartoons are most violent?
- Are there scientific research studies that have observed children before and after watching violent cartoons?
- Which major groups are involved in investigating this question? Which might agree with my thesis? Which would not?

Now, let's play: Is It a Thesis?

Choose the best thesis statement in each of the following four pairs of statements. Consider how you might improve these statements.

All men are chauvinists

> Our American family structure encourages middle-class men to repress their true feelings, leaving them open to physical, psychological, and relationship difficulties.

Steroid abuse negatively affects sports

> Steroids, even those legally available, should be banned from college sports because they are addictive, unhealthy, and essentially unfair.

Hip-hop is the best thing that has happened to music in twenty years

> Though many people dismiss hip-hop as offensive, hip-hop music offers urban youth an important opportunity for artistic expression and allows them to articulate the poetry of the street.

Many people object to today's violent horror movies

> Despite their high-tech special effects, today's graphically violent horror movies do not convey the impact and level of emotion that we saw in the classic horror films of the 1940s and 1950s.

Your turn. Now let's work together to develop thesis statements around areas in which we already have some background knowledge. Here are a few ideas: high-school sports, school uniforms, high-stakes testing, steroid abuse, divorce, school dances, music censorship.

Does your preliminary thesis pass the following tests? Does it:

- inspire the reader to ask "how?" or "why?"
- avoid statements that no one will react to, or statements that a reasonable reader will react to with a sarcastic "No kidding!" or "Who cares?"
- avoid general or extreme words or phrases?
- lead the reader toward logical subtopics?
- lend itself to being adequately developed in the required length of the project?

FROM TOPIC TO THESIS: WALKING THROUGH THE PROCESS

thesis

topic

An effective thesis unifies and structures your project's content and organization. Develop a good one and you're halfway there!

Sample Topic: School Uniforms

STEP 1: Attempt to narrow your topic; if you can't at this point, that's okay.

Examples: School uniforms in public schools

School uniforms in suburban public schools

School uniforms in our high school

STEP 2: Brainstorm all the possible questions you can think of about your topic.

- Get a partner to help you—let your mind be free to explore anything related to the topic.
- Be careful not to let your bias toward the topic get in the way of brainstorming.

STEP 3: Brainstorm any arguments related to your topic.

Examples: School uniforms: What are the pros and cons?

Why? Why not? How? Where?

Under what circumstances?

Who benefits from school uniforms, and how?

Where has it worked? Where hasn't it worked and why?

Is there research to prove their effectiveness?

What are the factors involved at our school?

STEP 4: Take a stance or position.

- Begin with considering the positive or negative. Are you for or against the topic/concept/practice?

  Examples: I am for school uniforms at our school.

  I am against school uniforms at our school.

  I don't know right now how I feel, but I am leaning toward . . .

  I have no idea.

- What are your reasons for being for or against?
- Using a t-chart, brainstorm all the possible reasons for and against.
- Keep this chart handy as you do your research to add reasons you might not have thought about originally.

Remember to *keep an open mind.* There is likely to be much you have yet to learn. Decide on a question or a couple of questions to guide your research:

Example: Would mandating school uniforms for all students at our school have beneficial effects academically and socially?

An effective thesis should pass the following five tests. It should:

- frame the statement so it inspires the reader to ask "How?" or "Why?"
- avoid statements that no one will react to, or that a reasonable reader will react to with a sarcastic "No kidding!" or "Who cares?"
- avoid general or extreme words or phrases.
- lead the reader toward your subtopics.
- be adequately developed in the required length of the project.

Do these statements pass the five effectiveness tests?

Examples: School uniforms should be mandated clothing.

School uniforms are a bad idea.

School uniforms at Springfield HS will kill creativity and individuality.

Mandating school uniforms for grades 8–12 in Springfield High School will result in increased academic performance.

Even if mandated school uniforms at SHS do not result in higher academic performance, other benefits make it worthwhile.

Try Developing Your Own Thesis

Remember, you can always modify your thesis, but what you begin with guides your research.

Topic_____

Brainstorm questions related to topic:

(Continued)

From Topic to Thesis: Walking through the Process (Continued)

Brainstorm what you know about the pro and con sides:

Pro	Con

Take a tentative stance:

Apply the "tests":

Now, research with a directed but open mind! Record any important knowledge that would help you refine your thesis statement here or in your t-chart:

Revise your thesis according to research:

Developed and contributed by Carol H. Rohrbach, language arts coordinator, School District of Springfield Township, Erdenheim, Pa.

BOOLEAN AEROBICS

This activity will help you understand how the AND, OR, and NOT operators are used to broaden or narrow a search.

The AND Workout

Stand up if you have brown hair.

Remain standing if you have brown hair AND brown eyes.

Remain standing if you have brown hair AND brown eyes AND are wearing glasses.

Remain standing if you have brown hair AND brown eyes AND are wearing glasses AND are wearing black shoes.

Questions or Ideas?

- Did AND make your search bigger or smaller?
- How would you use AND in a search?

The OR Workout

Stand up if you have brown hair.

Stand up if you have brown hair OR wear glasses (or contacts).

Questions or Ideas?

- Did OR make your search bigger or smaller?
- How would you use OR in a search?

The NOT Workout

Stand up if you have brown hair.

Stand up if you have brown hair but NOT brown eyes.

Questions or Ideas?

- Did NOT make your search bigger or smaller?
- How would you use NOT in a search?

"3M" CHART

Must	Might	Mustn't

Use this chart to plan your search.

- List in the *Must* column, the most important words or phrases related to your topic.
- List in the *Might* column, words or phrases you suspect might appear in a relevant result. (You may pick up more of these as you continue to search!)
- List in the *Mustn't* column, trouble words, words that may "throw off" the meaning of your search.
- Try to plan your search strategies as you fill in the chart. Put your phrases in quotes. Use wildcards (*) when you want to include plurals or other forms of a word you plan to use.

See the sample below for ideas.

Example: What are the major threats to the habitat of eagles in our country?

Must	Might	Mustn't
eagle*	bird*	Philadelphia
endanger*	raptor*	football
habitat	"North America"	
threat*	"United States"	

"3M" Chart by Bernard J. Dodge, Ph.D., San Diego State University

BEFORE YOU LOGON: PLANNING YOUR SEARCH

Sample question: How effective are drug abuse prevention programs for young people?

	CONNECT WITH "ANDS"			
	Concept #1	**Concept #2**	**Concept #3**	**Concept #4**
OR	teen*	"drug abuse"	prevention	effective*
OR	adolesc*	marijuana	programs	success
OR	children	alcohol	treatment	

Potential problem words (if any) to exclude or "NOT": medic*, prescription

Plan your own search using the strategies outlined above. Consider Boolean operators, phrases, and truncation. Remember to brainstorm synonyms or related words.

Question:

	CONNECT WITH "ANDS"			
	Concept #1	**Concept #2**	**Concept #3**	**Concept #4**
OR				
OR				
OR				

Potential problem words (if any) to exclude or "NOT":

SEARCH TOOL SPECIES: A FIELD GUIDE

There's a jungle of search options out there! To help you choose the right species for your information needs, here's a field guide. (Remember, you'll often want to use a combination of search tools.)

Search Engines

Search engines offer a *keyword approach* to searching. Search engines are *large* databases of web documents that rely on *robots, spiders,* or *crawlers,* automated programs that match words and phrases to web documents, ignoring certain common "stop words" like "the," "of," "a," and "an." Search engines depend on *you* to do the work through the use of *syntax,* which is the particular protocol, or the searching language, of each unique search engine.

Advantages

Search engines are large and offer broad databases of information. Good searchers can use strategies to create focused searches that will likely yield excellent results. Some "smarter" search engines use technologies to move high-quality, relevant results up to the first few pages of your results lists.

Which are the smarter search engines?

- Google offers "link relevance," or PageRank technology, to move the sites people link to most to the top of your list.
- Several newer search engines "autocategorize," or group, results into subject hierarchies or concept clusters. These include Teoma, WiseNut, or Vivísimo (really a meta-search engine). Some of these new search engines combine two or more of these "smart" features.
- Oingo uses a thesaurus to "disambiguate" terms with multiple meanings, like "china" or "java."

Disadvantages

Search engines do little original thinking. They match the words and phrases you enter with little regard for the meaning of those terms, the synonyms you forgot to mention, or the words you meant to exclude. They make no use of humans to organize or evaluate results.

Searchers often get many irrelevant results in their first several pages. Search engines calculate relevance in a variety of ways. "Pay for placement" policies put lots of advertising in front of searchers and may unfairly alter the real relevance of results. Searchers need to learn the strategies and the relevance habits behind their favorite search engines.

Use a search engine:

- when you have a narrow topic or several keywords
- when you want to do a comprehensive search
- when you want to retrieve a large number of documents on your topic
- when you want to search for particular types of documents, file types, source locations, languages, date last modified, etc.
- when you want to take advantage of newer retrieval technologies, such as concept clustering/autocategorization, popularity ranking, link ranking, thesauri

Examples of Search Engines

- Google http://google.com
- AllTheWeb http://alltheweb.com
- AltaVista http://altavista.com
- Hotbot http://hotbot.com
- Teoma http://teoma.com
- WiseNut http://wisenut.com

Meta-Search Engines

Meta-search engines have no databases of their own. They search across the databases of a variety of other search tools. More advanced meta-search engines collate your results and eliminate repetitive hits. Some combine results into one unified list; others report each search engine's results separately.

Advantages

Meta-search tools offer a comprehensive search, an opportunity to take a broad look at what types of materials are out there on the Web. Some meta-search engines offer searches across databases you yourself would ordinarily overlook. Some allow you to conveniently search all your favorite search engines in one blow.

Disadvantages

Bigger is not always better. Meta-search engines sometimes ignore more sophisticated search strategies. Search protocol is not standardized across search tools. When you search with a familiar search engine, you get to know how to exploit its particular syntax. Meta-search tools may take a little more time to display results. Because of the greater processing time required, you may get only partial results in the time it would have taken to get full results in a standard search engine. Most meta-search engines limit the time they spend at each database and return only a small percentage of results from each of the search tools queried. Some meta-search tools lock you in their own frames. In order to see the URLs of the results you want to visit, you must figure out how to toggle out of frames.

Use a meta-search engine:

- when you have failed to find what you are looking for in your favorite search tools
- when you don't feel you need to use complex search strategies
- when you want to get a feel for "what's out there" on a particular topic

A word of advice: If the results of your meta-search are overwhelming, or mostly irrelevant, go back to using the individual search tools.

Examples of Meta-Search Engines

- Vivísimo http://vivisimo.com/
- ProFusion http://www.profusion.com
- Query Server http://www.queryserver.com/
- Dogpile http://www.dogpile.com
- Ixquick http://www.ixquick.com

Subject Directories

Subject directories are catalogs of websites collected, organized, and maintained by *humans,* not robots or spiders. Directories are usually arranged in "trees," or hierarchies, which attempt to organize information into large and progressively smaller subcategories. Subject directory editors generally review and select sites for inclusion based on established criteria. Subject directories base their databases on a thesaurus of terms. When directory editors index, they consider synonyms, linking together words like "car" and "automobile." Directories vary in type. To judge the usefulness of a subject directory, consider who selects and categorizes its resources, how its results are displayed, and whether its results are ranked, reviewed, or annotated.

Advantages

Though they may offer fewer results than search engines, subject directories return results that are generally of high quality and high relevance. They may offer valuable annotations and the ability to browse among related materials.

Disadvantages

Directories are much smaller in scope than search engines. Unlike search engines, directories do not store databases of websites, but merely point to them. They search their own database structures. Although this may limit results to higher-quality links, it may also take a while for directory editors to recognize changes and the disappearance of links. Dead links are a drawback for many directories.

Tip: When you need to combine several concepts, or if you are looking for something very specific, you are better off starting in a search engine.

Use a subject directory:

- when you are just starting out and want to examine a few quality sites
- when you have a broad topic or one major keyword or concept
- when you want to get quickly to the best sites on a topic
- when you are looking for a group of similar sites on the same topic
- when you want annotations before you visit sites
- when subject headings would be useful to regroup or retrieve relevant material
- when you want to avoid viewing "noise" documents frequently picked up by search engines

(Continued)

Examples of Subject Directories

- Google Directory http://directory.google.com
- LookSmart http://looksmart.com
- Yahoo! http://yahoo.com
- About.com http://about.com

MORE-ACADEMIC DIRECTORIES

- Librarians' Index to the Internet http://lii.org
- WWW Virtual Library http://vlib.org/Overview.html
- INFOMINE http://infomine.ucr.edu/

Invisible or Deep Web

"Invisible Web" or "Deep Web" are terms used to describe the huge amount of web content that is difficult or impossible to find using traditional search tools. This content includes databases, special file types (like PDFs and spreadsheets), and other sites that require password access, and sites that block robots or spiders.

How to Find the Invisible Web

- Use a standard search tool and enter your search terms and the term "database."
- Search Librarians' Index to the Internet or INFOMINE, and pay particular attention to the results labeled "database."
- Browse through special topical indexes designed especially for the Invisible Web.
- Use the subscription databases offered by your school and public libraries—EBSCOhost, GaleNet, FACTS.com, WilsonWeb, CQ Researcher, LexisNexis, etc.

Directories for the Invisible Web

- Invisible Web Directory http://invisible-web.net/
- SearchIQ http://invisible-web.net/
- InvisibleWeb.com http://www.invisibleweb.com/
- IncyWincy http://www.incywincy.com/
- Geniusfind http://www.geniusfind.com/
- CompletePlanet http://completeplanet.com
- Fossick http://fossick.com

Examples of Invisible Web Databases

- GEM: Gateway to Educational Materials http://thegateway.org
- Internet Movie Database http://imdb.com
- Healthfinder http://www.healthfinder.gov/
- Artchive http://www.artchive.com

Examples of Other Types of Special Search Tools

NEWS SEARCH ENGINES

- AltaVista News http://news.altavista.com/
- CNN.com http://cnn.com
- Daypop http://www.daypop.com/
- HeadlineSpot.com http://headlinespot.com
- RocketNews http://rocketnews.com/
- Worldnews.com http://worldnews.com
- Yahoo! News http://news.yahoo.com/
- Find Articles.com http://www.findarticles.com/
- MagPortal http://magportal.com

IMAGE/MEDIA SEARCHING

- AltaVista Image Finder http://www.altavista.com/cgi-bin/query?mmdo=1&stype=simage
- Google Image Search http://images.google.com/
- Ditto.com: The Place for Pictures http://www.ditto.com/
- Find Sounds http://www.findsounds.com/
- Fossick.com Multimedia Fossick.com http://fossick.com/Multimedia.htm
- Hotbot http://www.hotbot.com
- Lycos Richmedia http://richmedia.lycos.com/
- Pics4Learning http://pics.tech4learning.com/pics/index.htm
- PicSearch http://picsearch.com
- Proteus Image Search (combined search interface) http://www.thrall.org/proimage.html
- Yahoo Picture Gallery http://gallery.yahoo.com/
- Yahoo News Image Gallery http://dailynews.yahoo.com/h/g/ts/

PRACTICING SEARCH STRATEGIES

The good news is that most search engines allow you to use such powerful features as Boolean operators (AND, OR, NOT), phrase searching, and truncation to help you move the best resources toward the top of your results lists. The bad news is that each search engine may use different syntax, or search language, to accomplish that goal.

Though you will find some results searching carelessly, you will improve your results if you develop the habit of using solid strategies. For each of these test searches, select a search tool from among Google, AllTheWeb, and AltaVista, and describe the search strategy you would use for one of these tools. Be creative and, if you dare, give the advanced search screens a try!

Hint: You will absolutely need to refer to the "help" or "search tips" sheet for each search engine to complete this assignment. You might also want to refer to Danny Sullivan's chart of Search Engine Features at http://searchenginewatch.com/facts/ataglance.html.

Extra credit: Which of these search engines allow natural language?

---

1. Is there a risk of carpal tunnel syndrome for young people who play video games excessively?

SEARCH TOOL SELECTED:

SEARCH EXPRESSION:

---

2. Should hip-hop music be taken seriously as poetry?

SEARCH TOOL SELECTED:

SEARCH EXPRESSION:

---

3. Where are the best places to see dolphins on my vacation to Florida?

SEARCH TOOL SELECTED:

SEARCH EXPRESSION:

---

4. Are school cliques harmful to teenage girls?

SEARCH TOOL SELECTED:

SEARCH EXPRESSION:

---

5. What diseases pose the most serious risks to canines?

SEARCH TOOL SELECTED:

SEARCH EXPRESSION:

FOCUSING A TOPIC FOR RESEARCH

Student name _____ Teacher _____ Period _____

Broad topic or essential question to research:

Before you begin your research, brainstorm and list

Keywords:

Related words, names, places:

Subtopics:

Questions:

Database strategies: List the search engines, subject directories, databases, and types of print resources you plan to search.

After searching: List the three most promising sources you found and the engine or database that led you to each.

1.

2.

3.

After initial research: Frame a thoughtful question or preliminary thesis statement that you now feel is interesting or worthy of researching. Be careful to avoid a "so what" question or thesis.

Reflect: How did the search go? Which sources appear to be most useful? Do you need to further refine this topic before deciding on a preliminary thesis or question to drive your research?

PRACTICE FOCUSING A TOPIC

Use before and while searching and feel free to substitute your own potential topics.

CENSORSHIP

Related terms:

Subtopics:

Questions/Preliminary Thesis to explore (what I wonder about, predict, believe, propose):

GENETIC ENGINEERING

Related terms:

Subtopics:

Questions/Preliminary Thesis to explore (what I wonder about, predict, believe, propose):

SCHOOL VIOLENCE

Related terms:

Subtopics:

Questions/Preliminary Thesis to explore (what I wonder about, predict, believe, propose):

SEARCHQUEST: A WEBQUEST ABOUT SEARCH TOOLS

This activity is designed as an antidote to student "search tool rut"; to introduce students to the vast array of search engines, subject directories, and meta-search engines available to them; and to alert them to the idea that each may offer different features and employ different syntax.

A major contest, "the Searchies," is under way to determine the best search tools. Student groups will become expert in one search tool and demonstrate it by creating a commercial "selling" its best features to the class. Depending on time, the presentations may be informal or they may be formal multimedia events. After all, these tools are products competing with one another for the attention of information consumers. Following all the "commercial" presentations, the class will rank the search tools and award them specific honors.

The following page is a student handout. Use it to guide students in collecting relevant information for their commercials.

The complete unit, assessment tool, and advice for teachers are posted online at http://mciu.org/~spjvweb/sqstu.html.

SEARCH TOOL ORGANIZER

Use this chart to help you record the features you'll be demonstrating in your commercial. Pay particular attention to the starred items.

Search Tool _____ URL _____	Notes
TYPE OF TOOL: __ Search engine __ Subject directory __ Meta-search engine	
SEARCH STRATEGIES: Which Boolean operators can you use? How do you express "AND"?	
OTHER SEARCH STRATEGIES: Is phrase searching allowed? How? Are there special strategies for name searching? Is the search tool case-sensitive?	
SPECIALIZED SEARCHES: Can you search for images, audio, video, etc.?	
*SPECIAL FEATURES: What unique tricks does this search tool perform?	
*RESULTS: How are they arranged? How are they ranked? Are there summaries or annotations? Who wrote them?	
If your tool is a search engine, is there also a *subject directory?* (See *Search Tool Species: A Field Guide.*)	
*SMALL PRINT: What's missing here? Are there negative features?	

What are the five major selling points for this search tool?
1.

2.

3.

4.

5.

THE BIG DECISION: SUBJECT OR KEYWORD SEARCHING

subject? keyword?

One of your first steps in the search process is deciding whether to use a keyword or subject approach. When you are searching a subscription database, like EBSCOhost or GaleNet, or an online encyclopedia, these choices are clearly marked. If you are searching the Web, this decision is equivalent to choosing between a search engine (keyword) and a subject directory (topic). For each of the following examples, decide which would be the *best* search approach and underline the words you would choose as search terms. You may write-in terms of your own.

Note: When one search approach doesn't work, try the other!

1. The effect of cliques on middle-school girls

   Topic _____ Keyword _____

2. Greek mythology

   Topic _____ Keyword _____

3. The age of the dinosaurs

   Topic _____ Keyword _____

4. Information about martial arts

   Topic _____ Keyword _____

5. The impact of television violence on children

   Topic _____ Keyword _____

6. Censorship and women in rap music

   Topic _____ Keyword _____

7. Should humans be cloned?

   Topic _____ Keyword _____

8. X-treme sports

   Topic _____ Keyword _____

9. Children of the Holocaust

   Topic _____ Keyword _____

10. Hurricane tracking and prediction

    Topic _____ Keyword _____

VISUALIZING THE SEARCH PROCESS

Planning/Thinking	Searching	Refining/Evaluating

Identifying the problem

Essential questions?
How much information
do I need?
What type of information
do I need?
(primary sources?
magazine articles?
reference?)
Point of view?

Refining the problem

Are my questions too
broad? Too narrow?
Did I discover better
questions as I searched?
Are my results
comprehensive?
Balanced? Readable?
Of high quality?
Should I seek
adult advice?

**Selecting appropriate
search tools**

Search engines?
Subject directories?
Subscription databases?
Invisible Web?
Experts?
OPAC?

**Refining search
tool choices**

Did I select the
right databases?
Are there others left to try?
Print resources I
should consider?
Should I seek
adult advice?

**Developing search
strategies**

Brainstorming
keywords, synonyms,
related words?
Boolean strategies?
Phrases?
Considering the syntax
of selected
search tools?

**Refining search
strategies**

Were my strategies
effective?
Should I refer to tip sheets?
Advanced screens?
Have I found additional
keywords or concepts?
Do I need
to revise spelling?
Should I seek
adult advice?

These steps are not necessarily performed in exact order. Searching Is Cyclical! Searching Is Interactive! Reconsider questions and revise your strategies as you respond to your results. Good searchers use a variety of search tools as well as print sources.

POWER SEARCHING TIPS FOR THE WEB AND ONLINE DATABASES

If you are not happy with your results, try another search engine or database; check your spelling; or try synonyms or related, broader, or narrower terms. By all means, use some strategy. Though they have many quirks, most engines allow users the following advanced techniques. Check the "search tips," "cheat sheet," or "help" pages for the proper way to express these strategies.

Boolean Operators	
+, AND	limits your search, requiring that all words appear Vietnam AND protest AND students +Japan +cooking +eagles +habitat +endangered
OR	is used to capture synonyms or related words car OR automobile coronary OR heart
-, NOT, AND NOT	eliminates possibilities that you suspect will cause problems Martin Luther NOT King +eagles -Philadelphia -football
Most search engines allow you to use "+" and "-" for AND and NOT. These characters must appear immediately before your search terms. Do not separate them with spaces. Note: Google always assumes an AND!	
Wildcards, Truncation, Stemming	Many search tools and databases allow you to use an asterisk (*) to stand for any character or string of characters. This method is especially useful if you are uncertain of spelling or if you want to pick up varying forms of a word. Some search tools allow you to use a question mark (?) to substitute for *one* character, either in the middle of a word or at the end. teen* (picks up teenage, teenagers, or teens) Herz* (for Herzegovina) wom?n (for woman or women) s?ng (for sing, sang, sung)
Phrases	You often will want words to appear together in a specific order. Quotation marks ("") set words off as phrases to be searched as a whole. "vitamin A" "raisin in the sun" "George Washington Carver"
Proximity	Words are often not meaningful in a search unless they appear near each other in a document. In large documents, words separated by lots of text are generally unrelated. NEAR/25 specifies that two words appear within 25 words of each other (used in AltaVista, AOL Search, and Lycos) Eric Clapton NEAR/10 Cream

Field Searching	This strategy restricts searches to certain portions of web documents. It allows you to specify that search terms appear, for instance, in the title or URL of your results (used in a variety of ways in AltaVista, AllTheWeb, and Google).
	
	    title:cancer
	    URL:epa
	    domain:edu +"graphic organizers"
	    inurl:nasa (used in Google)

Case Sensitivity	Most search engines are case insensitive by default, that is, they treat uppercase and lowercase letters the same. However, there are some that recognize uppercase and lowercase variations. It is good practice to search using lowercase letters unless you have a specific strategy in mind. In case-sensitive search tools:
	
	    Baker (retrieves name and eliminates most references to cake and
	        bread makers)
	    AIDS (eliminates references to helpers)
	    China (eliminates references to dishes)

Combining Strategies	Check to see if the search tool allows you to combine strategies. For example, you might find it helpful to combine Boolean operators. Use parentheses ( ) to nest, or group, your ORs and ANDs in more sophisticated searching. As in algebra, what's in parentheses gets processed first.
	
	    +dolphins +(behavior OR behaviour) –miami
	Example using Google syntax:
	    inurl:nasa +saturn

Searching within Your Search	If you have a long results list, and even if you don't, you might choose to search for targeted words within your search. Several search engines offer a handy feature to help you narrow your results lists. After you perform your first search, look for a "search within results" feature. If no such feature exists, you can use your browser's own "find" feature to search the text of each page.
Natural Language Searches	Some search engines (Ask Jeeves, for instance) allow you to type questions as you would think or speak them. "Why is the sky blue?"

Tip about tips: Every search engine is slightly different. For instance, Google uses an automatic AND. Some search engines allow for "natural language" searching. Remember to carefully read the "tips page" of the search tools you use most frequently. This page discusses the syntax, or the specific search language, used by that particular search engine or directory.

WHY A SUBJECT DIRECTORY? (HIGH SCHOOL)

Students love search engines. But subject directories are very often the best place to begin a search, especially when you are searching for one concept, when you have some very general keywords, or when you're just beginning your research. At that point, you may not know enough about a topic to narrow it down.

Let's put subject directories to the test on some very common school searches. For each subject, how many truly relevant hits do you find on the first page or two of your results list?

	SUBJECT DIRECTORIES		SEARCH ENGINES	
	Librarians' Index to the Internet http://lii.org	Google Directory http://directory. google.com	AltaVista http://altavista.com	AllTheWeb http://alltheweb.com
Civil War (U.S.)				
Black history				
Refugees				
Child labor				
Jazz				

WHY A SUBJECT DIRECTORY? (MIDDLE/INTERMEDIATE SCHOOL)

Students love search engines. But subject directories are very often the best place to begin a search, especially when you are searching for one concept, when you have some very general keywords, or when you're just beginning your research. At that point, you may not know enough about a topic to narrow it down.

Let's put subject directories to the test on some very common school searches. For each subject, how many truly relevant hits do you find on the first page or two of your results list?

| | SUBJECT DIRECTORIES | | SEARCH ENGINES | |
	KidsClick! http://sunsite.berkeley.edu/ KidsClick!/	Awesome Library for Kids http://www.awesomelibrary. org/student.html	AltaVista http://altavista.com	AllTheWeb http://alltheweb.com
Dinosaurs				
Black history				
Pennsylvania				
Insects				
Orchestra				

27

WEB SCAVENGER HUNT

This activity will acquaint you with our library's online database resources and the standard reference tools and information gateways of the Web.

Choose from links on the Resource Page to help you answer the questions. Create a word-processed document to record your answers. Staple any requested printouts to this document.

1. Use one of our library's subscription magazine databases to find an article on the cloning of humans. Create a citation for this article. (Use our MLA style sheet to guide you.)

2. Use MapQuest.com to determine how many miles it is from Portland, Oregon, to Portland, Maine. How many hours would it take to drive the distance?

3. Use an online almanac to determine who is the oldest:

   Michael Jackson

   Michael Jordan

   Michael J. Fox

   Cite your source!

4. Use an online almanac to determine the three deadliest tornadoes in the United States. List where they occurred, their dates, and the number of fatalities. Cite your source.

5. Use the CIA World Factbook (http://www.odci.gov/cia/publications/factbook/index.html) to find a map of Argentina. Paste the map into your word-processing document and cite it as an image.

6. Use the U.S. Department of State Background Notes or the Library of Congress Country Studies sites to find three little-known facts about the history of Afghanistan.

7. Use one of the sites in the preceding two questions to find out the status of suffrage in Saudi Arabia.

8. Use your favorite search tool to find the home page for the United States Senate. Who are the current two senators from our state? What is the current Congress called?

9. What is today's temperature in Fairbanks, Alaska?

10. What is the top news story in our local newspaper?

11. Using our library's online catalog (OPAC), search for a book about a historic event you find interesting. Record the citation for the book.

12. Use an online encyclopedia to find a biographical article about one of your heroes. What are the three most important contributions this person made?

13. Use the Occupational Outlook Handbook (http://www.bls.gov/oco/) to research a career you find interesting. Answer the following:

    What would you expect to earn in a year?
    What is the employment outlook for this field?

14. What are the five Ws for one of the lead stories in CNN.com today?

    Who?

    What?

    Where?

    When?

    Why?

15. Using your favorite search engine, do a search on child labor in the world. Print the first page of your results list, circle the best result, and offer a reason for why that result is the best. Why did you choose that result?

16. Using a subject directory, locate a high-quality website on the Civil War in the United States. Which subject directory did you use? Why did you choose that particular site?

17. Describe, in your own words, the difference between a search engine and a subject directory.

18. Use an image search tool to locate a photograph of your favorite sports star. Cite the image as you would in a school project. (Paste the picture and type the citation into your word-processed document.)

19. According to MLA Online (http://www.mla.org), how do you quote a source from the Web in your paper if websites generally have no page numbers?

20. Use the Internet Movie Database (http://imdb.com) to find a review of your favorite film. Cite one of the external reviews and quote one comment by the reviewer.

RESOURCE PAGE FOR WEB SCAVENGER HUNT

Our own online library resources:

Access to our OPAC _____

MLA Online style sheet _____

Magazine and journal indexes: Our library provides access to the full text of magazines and newspapers through subscription databases. You can access them from our homepage or directly here _____.

General Reference Sources

MapQuest http://www.mapquest.com

CIA World Factbook http://www.odci.gov/cia/publications/factbook/index.html

U.S. Department of State Background Notes http://www.state.gov/r/pa/bgn/

Occupational Outlook Handbook http://www.bls.gov/oco/

MLA Online http://www.mla.org

Internet Movie Database http://imdb.com

Almanacs

Fact Monster http://www.factmonster.com

Information Please http://www.infoplease.com

World Almanac for Kids http://www.worldalmanacforkids.com

Online Encyclopedias

Library subscriptions to full encyclopedias: _____
Free web-based encyclopedias:

Britannica http://www.britannica.com/

Encarta (Concise) http://encarta.msn.com/

Encyclopedia Proteus (combined search) http://rtiess.tripod.com/proteus/encyclopedia.htm

Selected Search Engines

Google http://google.com

AllTheWeb http://alltheweb.com

Teoma http://teoma.com

AltaVista http://altavista.com

WiseNut http://wisenut.com

Hotbot http://hotbot.com

Vivísimo (meta-search) http://vivisimo.com

Selected Subject Directories

Librarians' Index to the Internet http://lii.org

Google Directory http://directory.google.com

About.com http://about.com

WWW Virtual Library http://vlib.org/Overview.html

Yahoo! http://yahoo.com

Image Search Tools

AltaVista Image Finder http://www.altavista.com/cgi-bin/query?mmdo=1&stype=simage

Google Image Search http://images.google.com/

Corbis.com http://corbis.com/

Ditto.com: The Place for Pictures http://www.ditto.com/

Hotbot http://www.hotbot.com

Lycos Richmedia http://richmedia.lycos.com/

Pics4Learning http://pics.tech4learning.com/pics/index.htm

PicSearch http://picsearch.com

Proteus Image Search (combined search interface) http://www.thrall.org/proimage.html

Yahoo Picture Gallery http://gallery.yahoo.com/

Yahooligans! Downloader http://www.yahooligans.com/Downloader/

Weather Information

Accuweather http://www.accuweather.com/weatherf/index_corp

Intellicast.com http://www.intellicast.com/

National Weather Service http://www.nws.noaa.gov/

United States Weather Pages http://www.uswx.com/us/wx

Weather.com (Weather Channel) http://www.weather.com

Weather Underground http://www.wunderground.com/

USING EXPERTS AS INFORMATION SOURCES

Ask me!

One of the greatest advantages of researching on the Web is the access to people it provides. You now have access to experts in almost any field of knowledge. Official expert sites offer gateway access to these people. Unofficially, you might examine the very best websites relating to your topic and look for email addresses of the authors or webmasters.

Before you write an email to an expert, consider the following tips:

- Introduce yourself politely.
- Explain how you were led to the person.
- Describe your purpose. Ask a simple, direct question.
- Mention any deadline.
- Describe what you have already accomplished in your research.
- Respect the expert's time.
- Politely thank the person in advance for any help or other leads he or she might be able to offer.
- Remember, don't offer any personal information in your email (phone number, street address).
- If you get any response, follow up with a note of thanks.

Expert Gateway Sites

- Abuzz (New York Times Knowledge Sharing) http://www.abuzz.com
- Allexperts.com (About.com) http://www.allexperts.com/
- Ask a Scientist http://scorescience.humboldt.k12.ca.us/fast/ask.htm
- Ask an Expert Page http://www.k12science.org/askanexpert.html
- Virtual Reference Desk Ask A+ Locator http://www.vrd.org/locator/subject.shtml
- KidsConnect (Ask a school librarian) send email to AskKC@ala.org or http://www.ala.org/ICONN/kidsconn.html
- Ask Dr. Math http://mathforum.org/dr.math/

A Sample Email Message

Dear Ms. Helpful,

I am a tenth-grade student studying the use of Excel in accounting for my Programming class. I have already found material in the Occupational Outlook Handbook and examined journal articles from the business databases. I am hoping you might be able to help me understand how this software is used in your industry by answering the following questions:

[List specific questions here. Do not ask a busy expert to tell you "everything" he or she knows about a very general topic.]

I appreciate any help you might be able to offer. My project is due on May 28, 2003.

Thank you,
Sally Student

Using Experts: Electronic Discussion Lists and Usenet Groups

Beyond the world of actual web pages, there is a whole lot of discussion going on. Professionals or specialists within a field carry on serious discussions through their mailing lists and newsgroups.

Electronic Discussion Lists/Mailing Lists

One effective way to find information on the Web is to actually listen in or, very carefully, join the discussion. By now you've probably heard of, or may actually belong to, a mailing list. Communities are the core of the Internet. They are unprecedented sources of information, links to experts and professionals, and ways to identify the movers and shakers in any particular field.

How do you find these lists? Of course, there are gateways.

Among the most comprehensive of the gateways to the mailing list communities is Topica (http://www.topica.com), which offers a directory of well over 90,000 Internet mailing lists.

Getting information from the members of an electronic discussion list is a bit more complicated than searching a standard search tool. You may need to schedule some time before you even get to ask a question. First, you'll need to identify the most appropriate community. Then, you'll need to "lurk" a bit to discover the list's culture and the protocols.

A little advice about asking questions of discussion list members:

- Be brief and clear and respectful.
- Identify yourself and your purpose.
- Ask if the group might be able to identify an expert for you to email.
- Let the group know what you know, what resources you have already checked.

- Get rid of any silly screen name or signature files before asking a question in a serious group.
- Thank anyone who offers you help.

GATEWAY SITES FOR FINDING MAILING LISTS

- CataList, the catalog of LISTSERV lists http://www.lsoft.com/lists/listref.html
- Topica http://www.topica.com/
- PAML (Publicly Accessible Mailing Lists) http://paml.net/
- TileNet http://tile.net/lists/

Newsgroups or Usenet Groups

Like mailing lists or discussion lists, usenet groups are generally devoted to a specific interest. But unlike mailing lists, which automatically send email to your address, usenet group postings are accessed through a web browser. The major advantage to usenet groups is that they allow you to sort through a wide variety of postings without cluttering your mailbox. One of the disadvantages of usenet groups is that the discussion may be spottier and the quality of posts vary more than with mailing lists.

Google Groups is a huge, searchable collection of postings to usenet newsgroups, most available way back to 1995:

- Google Groups http://groups.google.com/

SEARCH PLANNER

Brainstorming Keywords

Question/Thesis:

+   or   +   or   +

or   or   or

+   or   +   or   +

Databases to search:

Descriptors found in searching:
Synonyms:

Broader/Narrower:

Proper nouns (names, places, organizations, companies):

Alternate spellings:

Preliminary/Working Thesis

Topic/Argument:	Topic/Argument:	Topic/Argument:
Evidence:	Evidence:	Evidence:

Working conclusion:

Promising Dewey (call) numbers:

Promising major websites:

2

Ethics

From *Information Power*

Social Responsibility

Standard 7: The student who contributes positively to the learning community and to society is information literate and recognizes the importance of information to a democratic society.

Indicators
1. Seeks information from diverse sources, contexts, disciplines, and cultures
2. Respects the principles of equitable access to information

Standard 8: The student who contributes positively to the learning community and to society is information literate and practices ethical behavior in regard to information and information technology.

Indicators
1. Respects the principles of intellectual freedom
2. Respects intellectual property rights
3. Uses information technology responsibly

From *NETS for Students*

2. Social, ethical, and human issues
   • Students understand the ethical, cultural, and societal issues related to technology.
   • Students practice responsible use of technology systems, information, and software.

- Students develop positive attitudes toward technology uses that support lifelong learning, collaboration, personal pursuits, and productivity.

From *Information Literacy Competency Standards for Higher Education* (Association of College and Research Libraries)

Standard 5: The information literate student understands many of the economic, legal, and social issues surrounding the use of information and accesses and uses information ethically and legally.

Performance Indicators

1. The information literate student understands many of the ethical, legal, and socioeconomic issues surrounding information and information technology.
2. The information literate student follows laws, regulations, institutional policies, and etiquette related to the access and use of information resources.
3. The information literate student acknowledges the use of information sources in communicating the product or performance.

RELATED POSTERS

Citing Your Online Sources

Information Technology Ethics

Try asking your students these questions: How would you feel if someone opened your locker and went through your personal things? How would you feel if someone read the letter you just wrote to your best friend or "borrowed" your term paper and presented it to the teacher as his or her original work? How would you feel if you discovered someone had spread untrue gossip about you all over the neighborhood or took a paycheck you had just earned right out of your pocket?

Of course, all these activities are disturbing. But it is far easier for students to understand the effects of unethical behavior when they take place in the real, or face-to-face, world. Things get a bit fuzzier in the virtual world. The same students who might not hesitate to copy a piece of software, cut and paste an essay together, or poke around in the desktop folders of others might have far higher standards for behavior in the face-to-face world. The perceived anonymity afforded by information technologies creates an environment where students may easily choose not to "do the right thing" either because they cannot see the harm they might do or because they sense no danger of getting caught.

We do not want to live in a world where cheating and unkind behavior are commonplace. Despite the anonymity students feel behind a workstation, despite the ease and convenience of electronic copying, it is *not* okay to copy software, hack into a network, publicly slander or humiliate, buy a term paper off the Web, cut and paste an essay, read someone else's email, or download copyrighted music and video.

In our homes, classrooms, and libraries, we are dealing with a wide array of ethical issues relating to information technology. We need to ensure that the values we instill in our children translate clearly to a virtual world. We can accomplish this goal by clearly articulating our principles and guidelines and by continually modeling, reinforcing, and encouraging discussion of ethical issues.

The Internet is a community in which real people communicate and do business. Networks and software are property. Insults and bad advice do harm even when you cannot see the person receiving them. We are compelled to focus our attention on cultivating academic integrity, indeed, human integrity, for the betterment of our students, to ensure that they will live in a civilized world, and simply because it's the right thing for us to do as educators.

ACTIVITIES AND HANDOUTS

Discouraging Plagiarism: This handout for teachers (see p. 37) describes strategies to discourage cut-and-paste, recycled, or purchased student projects.

Is It Plagiarism? A Discussion: This activity (see p. 38) asks students to personally consider whether several commonly observed behaviors constitute plagiarism. Following individual reflection, ask the whole class to discuss the situations. Among the less-obvious situations are items 4 (paraphrasing *does* require documentation) and 15 (whenever you take an image from the Web and publish it on your own page, unless otherwise specifically noted, you must not only cite the image but also get permission from the creator).

Ethics Questionnaire: Doug Johnson, director of media and technology for the Mankato (Minn.) Area Public Schools, developed this questionnaire (see p. 40) to inspire thoughtful discussions around the common, but serious, issues facing our students. Consider assigning individual scenarios to small groups for discussion before opening them up to the large group.

When Should I Document Sources in My Text? This handout (see p. 42) offers rules and examples for in-text citation.

Plagiarism versus Documentation: This handout (see p. 44) illustrates a variety of ways students might borrow ideas from text, ranging from obvious plagiarism to careful and ethical integration of text into original thought.

Documenting Your Sources: Based on MLA style, this handout (see p. 46) guides students in preparing Works Cited and Works Consulted pages for traditional sources.

Citing Online Sources: Documenting sources isn't as easy as it used to be. When you are working with websites, what do you do about page numbers in in-text documentation? What about those long URLs in databases? This handout (see p. 48), based on MLA style, will help students prepare Works Cited and Works Consulted pages, incorporating some of the most commonly used electronic sources.

Works Cited and Works Consulted Pages: Students are often confused by the two different lists we ask them to append to their projects. Use this handout (see p. 51), to explain why and when they should use each.

Source Cards: These source card samples (see p. 52) represent a few of the most-often cited resources. Photocopy the forms and have them available for students to use to record sources for their Works Cited or Works Consulted pages.

Note Cards: Have students use these note cards (see p. 54) to record quotations or paraphrases they'll later cite, making sure they carefully list sources and page numbers to match the references in their source cards.

Quoting, Paraphrasing, and Summarizing: It *is* okay to borrow from the works of others as long as students use the material responsibly. This handout (see p. 55), developed in collaboration with language arts coordinator Carol Rohrbach, explains how and when to credit others as students summarize, paraphrase, and quote.

Student Guidelines for Multimedia and Web Page Production: Students are likely to be confused about how much text or media they may borrow from other creators for their multimedia productions and about how to get permission to use material for web products. This handout (see p. 56), based on the *Fair Use Guidelines for Educational Multimedia,* offers advice on how much to use, how and when to cite, and how to get permissions.

Permission Letter Template: Our students' publications might reach well beyond the walls of our schools. Although a simple citation may be enough for a term paper or a PowerPoint presentation, the whole game changes when students publish on the Web or broadcast over the cable network. Post this letter template (see p. 58) on your web page or distribute it as a handout so that students might easily import or copy it into an email or a letter to obtain permission from a copyright owner.

Weaving Quotes into Your Writing: Springfield Township High School English teacher Ken Rodoff developed this exercise (see p. 59) to demonstrate how to effectively weave, not just paste, quotations into essays and papers. After asking students to read each writing sample, evaluate the sample as a group.

DISCOURAGING PLAGIARISM: ADVICE FOR TEACHERS

The best strategy for discouraging student plagiarism is effective assignment design.

The information landscape has changed, and areas of ethics are fuzzier than ever. Our students may not have a clear understanding of what constitutes plagiarism. In addition to traditional paper projects, students face new issues when they produce multimedia. Issues get even thornier when students publish their work on the Web.

Here are some additional strategies instructors can use to discourage plagiarism and promote higher-quality research:

- Do not assign topical research ("Do a report on California")! Ask students to compare, analyze, invent, propose, etc.

- Encourage inquiry-driven research. Have students pose thoughtful questions based on their preliminary reading.

- Emphasize both writing and research as processes.

- Require in-process assessments. Ask students to submit preliminary thesis statements, drafts of bibliographies, and outlines and organizers at various points in the process to avoid research catastrophes as well as plagiarism. Your librarian can help with these assessments.

- Build peer and instructor reactions into formative assessments.

- Confer with students at key points in the process.

- Require students to keep a journal about their experience with the research and writing processes.

- Require students to submit all drafts and outlines along with the final project.

- Require students to incorporate specific, appropriate, high-quality resources of varying types in the project. (For example, "Use two primary sources from Gale's *Student Resource Center*," or, for more advanced high-school students, "Use one scholarly journal.")

- Create an assignment-specific rubric that would not highly value a generic or recycled paper.

- Require students to attach a formal reflection piece, describing the research process, to their final project. Ask them to highlight what worked well and what were the greatest challenges, and to describe how they would change the process next time.

- Ask students to submit first pages (or entire documents) for any websites or sources not easily accessed through the library.

- Require an *annotated* bibliography. To simplify, you might ask students to annotate by noting the author's credentials and why the source was of particular value. Consider asking students to answer the following questions in their bibliographies:

  1. How did you find this information? Which database or search tool did you use?

  2. Who is the author and why should you trust him or her?

  3. Why is this particular document truly relevant to your thesis/research?

IS IT PLAGIARISM? A DISCUSSION

Plagiarism is theft of intellectual property. It is a form of cheating or stealing. If you present the work of others—words, images, sounds, ideas—as your own, you are plagiarizing. As students, your primary concerns should be learning and developing habits of scholarship.

The most obvious form of plagiarism is stealing an author's exact words and failing to use quotation marks or to cite the author. However, plagiarism can be far less obvious. Many students plagiarize unintentionally.

In order to be sure you avoid plagiarism, you'll need to have a clear idea of exactly what might be considered plagiarism. Have you ever done any of the things in the following list? Have you ever heard of anyone else actually doing any of these things? (No names, please.) Before we discuss these cases as a class, decide which of the following you would consider plagiarism. Some examples are clearer than others. Be ready to discuss your responses with the class.

1. Copying or sharing homework with a fellow student   Yes   No   Not Sure

   Comments:

2. Failing to cite a commonly known fact   Yes   No   Not Sure

   Comments:

3. Failing to cite a statistic   Yes   No   Not Sure

   Comments:

4. Paraphrasing without documenting the work of others you find in books, magazines, or websites   Yes   No   Not Sure

   Comments:

5. Asking another student to write a paper for you   Yes   No   Not Sure

   Comments:

6. Copying material from a source and citing the material in your bibliography, but leaving out in-text documentation   Yes   No   Not Sure

   Comments:

7. Listing works in your bibliography that you have not used or read   Yes   No   Not Sure

   Comments:

8. Mixing the words of an author with your own without documentation   Yes   No   Not Sure

   Comments:

9. Taking a paper you wrote for one class and submitting it to another teacher   Yes   No   Not Sure

   Comments:

10. Having your parent substantially edit your work   Yes   No   Not Sure

    Comments:

11. Copying and pasting relevant pieces of electronic text together, citing as you go along   Yes   No   Not Sure

    Comments:

12. Presenting a paper or document you found on the Internet as your own   Yes   No   Not Sure

    Comments:

13. Substantially editing a paper you found on the Internet   Yes   No   Not Sure

    Comments:

14. Pasting an image from a website into your multimedia project and documenting it   Yes   No   Not Sure

    Comments:

15. Pasting an image from a website into your web page and documenting it   Yes   No   Not Sure

    Comments:

ETHICS QUESTIONNAIRE

1. Adele meets Frank, who shares her interest in fig-ure skating, in an Internet chat room. After several conversations in the following weeks, Frank asks Adele for her home telephone number and address. Adele likes Frank and gives him the information he asked for. Is what Adele did:

    a) Right
    b) Wrong
    c) Sometimes right and sometimes wrong depending on the situation
    d) I don't know

2. The principal suspects Paul of using his school email account to send offensive messages to other stu-dents. He asks the network manager to give him copies of Paul's email. What the principal has done is

    a) Right
    b) Wrong
    c) Sometimes right and sometimes wrong depending on the situation
    d) I don't know

3. Helen is using the word processor on the class-room computer to keep her journal, but Mike keeps looking over her shoulder as she types. What Mike is doing is:

    a) Right
    b) Wrong
    c) Sometimes right and sometimes wrong depending on the situation
    d) I don't know

4. Ms. Eastman, Terry's teacher, needs to leave the room to take care of an emergency. While she is gone, Terry finds that Ms. Eastman had been work-ing on student progress reports and that her grading program is still open on her computer. He checks to see what grade he is getting and finds the grades for several other students. What Terry did is:

    a) Right
    b) Wrong
    c) Sometimes right and sometimes wrong depending on the situation
    d) I don't know

5. Jerry borrows Ben's game disks for *Monster Truck Rally II* and installs them on his home computer. He says he will erase the game if he does not like it, or will buy the game for himself if he likes it. Jerry has been using the game now for over a month and has not erased it from his computer and has not bought his own copy. Is Jerry's use of the game:

    a) Right
    b) Wrong
    c) Sometimes right and sometimes wrong depending on the situation
    d) I don't know

6. Cindy finds some good information about plant growth nutrients for her science fair project on a CD-ROM reference title. She uses the copy func-tion of the computer to take an entire paragraph from the CD-ROM article and paste it directly into her report. She writes down the title of the article and the CD-ROM from which it was taken. When she writes her report, she tells the source in her bibliography. Are Cindy's actions:

    a) Right
    b) Wrong
    c) Sometimes right and sometimes wrong depending on the situation
    d) I don't know

7. Albert finds a site on the Internet that is a collec-tion of old term papers for students to read and use. He downloads one on ancient Greece, changes the title, and submits it as his own. How Albert completed the assignment is:

    a) Right
    b) Wrong
    c) Sometimes right and sometimes wrong depending on the situation
    d) I don't know

8. Fahad is upset with his friend George. He finds the data disk on which George has been storing his essays and erases it. Fahad's actions are:

    a) Right
    b) Wrong
    c) Sometimes right and sometimes wrong depending on the situation
    d) I don't know

9. Henry's older friend Hank, a high school student, has discovered the password to the school's student information system. Because Hank feels a teacher has unfairly given him a poor grade, he plans to create a "bomb" which will erase all the information on the office computer. Henry tells his dad about Hank's plan. Are Henry's actions:

    a) Right
    b) Wrong
    c) Sometimes right and sometimes wrong depending on the situation
    d) I don't know

10. Jack's class has been using the digital camera to take pictures for the school yearbook. Jack has found that he can use a computer program to change the photographs. He has used the program so far to make himself look like the tallest boy in the class, to blacken out the front tooth of his best buddy who will think it is funny, and to give his teacher slightly crossed eyes. Jack's actions are:

    a) Right
    b) Wrong
    c) Sometimes right and sometimes wrong depending on the situation
    d) I don't know

11. Just for fun, thirteen-year-old Alice tells the other people on her electronic mailing list that she is twenty years old and a nursing student. Others on the list have begun emailing her health-related questions, but she hasn't answered them. Are Alice's actions:

    a) Right
    b) Wrong
    c) Sometimes right and sometimes wrong depending on the situation
    d) I don't know

12. As a joke, Chang sends an email message to his sister who attends a school across town. In this email he uses profanities and racial slurs. Are Chang's actions:

    a) Right
    b) Wrong
    c) Sometimes right and sometimes wrong depending on the situation
    d) I don't know

13. The computers in the library always seem to be busy. There is a rule that computers are used first by those with schoolwork. Otis tells the librarian he is working on a research project, but he also uses the computer to access the latest soccer scores posted on the Internet. Is Otis's behavior:

    a) Right
    b) Wrong
    c) Sometimes right and sometimes wrong depending on the situation
    d) I don't know

14. Just for fun, Nellie sets the print command on her computer to print 50 copies of an electronic encyclopedia article she's been reading, and then walks away. Are Nellie's actions:

    a) Right
    b) Wrong
    c) Sometimes right and sometimes wrong depending on the situation
    d) I don't know

15. Clark downloads a page with sexually explicit photographs from the Internet to a computer in the classroom. He shows its contents to others in his class. Are Clark's actions:

    a) Right
    b) Wrong
    c) Sometimes right and sometimes wrong depending on the situation
    d) I don't know

Reprinted with permission of Doug Johnson, director of media and technology, Mankato (Minn.) Area Public Schools <http://www.doug-johnson.com>

WHEN SHOULD I DOCUMENT SOURCES IN MY TEXT?

In-text (or in-project) documentation is the accepted format for acknowledging borrowed information within your original text. Footnotes are no longer frequently used, except in cases when you need to clarify or add information that might otherwise break the flow of your text or presentation.

Use in-text documentation to cite a source whenever you:

- use an original idea from one of your sources, whether you quote or paraphrase it
- summarize original ideas from one of your sources
- use factual information that is not common knowledge. (Common knowledge is information that recurs in many sources. If you are not certain it is common knowledge, cite to be safe.)
- quote directly from a source
- use a date, fact, or statistic that might be disputed

Usually only the author's last name and the page number or, in the absence of an author, the title and the page number are given. Do not use the word "page" or any abbreviations. Page numbers may be omitted if the article is a one-page document or is in an encyclopedia arranged alphabetically. Page numbers may also be omitted when citing web resources, which do not normally include paging.

The purpose of this format is to give immediate source information without interrupting the flow of the paper. Usually parenthetical citations are placed at the end of a sentence, but they may be placed in the middle (see example 6). The academic world takes in-text documentation seriously. Inaccurate documentation is as serious as having no documentation at all.

Rules for Using In-Text Documentation

1. Use the author's last name and give the page number in parentheses. Do not use the word "page" or abbreviations for "page"; just write the number. In most cases you will be citing one or two pages, leading your reader to a specific piece of information. Allow one space before the parentheses but none after if a period follows.

    Example: Arthur Miller's *The Crucible* "forces a revolution in our perception and definition of reality" (Martin 73).

2. If you are using more than one book by the same author, give the last name, comma, the title, and the page.

    Example: Animal imagery conveys the primitive, uncontrolled rage that the peasants feel. One person "acquired a tigerish smear about the mouth" (Dickens, *Tale of Two Cities* 33–34).

3. There is a relationship between your writing and how you compose your in-text documentation. If you identify the author and title in the text, you do not need to repeat that information; simply present the page number in your citation.

    Example: In *Understanding Why the Caged Bird Sings*, Megna-Wallace notes that Angelou's autobiography succeeds on two levels: "first, as a personal memoir . . . and second, as a representative narrative that exemplifies the struggle of many African American women against racial and sexual oppression" (10).

4. If there is no author, give the title and the page number.

   Example: A number of critics feel that Hemingway's journalistic style continued to influence writers through the end of the twentieth century ("Hemingway Chronicle" 5).

5. If you are using a direct quotation from a secondary source, you must identify it as such.

   Example: According to Arthur Miller, "It was not only McCarthyism that moved me, it was as though the whole country had been born anew, without a memory even of certain elemental decencies" (qtd. in Budick 74).

6. If a quotation or information appears in the middle of your own idea, then insert the documentation immediately after the quotation.

   Example: Arthur Miller's notion of a country "without a memory even of certain elemental decencies" (qtd. in Budick 74) resonates throughout *The Crucible*.

7. If the quoted material exceeds two lines in your text, use a comma or colon after the last word of text, indent, and type the quotation without quotation marks. The parenthetical citation follows the punctuation at the end of the last sentence of the quotation.

8. Web documents generally do not have fixed page numbers or any kind of section numbering. If your source lacks numbering, omit numbers from your in-text documentation and use only the main entry—author, or title, if there is no author—in parentheses.

   Note: For a web document, the page numbers of a printout should not be cited, because the pagination may vary in different printouts.

   Example: A recent CNN.com review noted that the book's purpose was "to teach cultures that are both different from and similar to world status quo" (Allen).

PLAGIARISM VERSUS DOCUMENTATION

Plagiarism is the act of presenting someone else's work as your own. It is the theft of intellectual property. The following examples should help you distinguish plagiarized research from well-documented research.

Original Text from David McCullough, *John Adams* (New York: Simon & Schuster, 2001), p. 57.

> His marriage to Abigail Smith was the most important decision of John Adams's life, as would become apparent with time. She was in all respects his equal and the part she was to play would be greater than he could possibly have imagined, for all his love for her and what appreciation he already had of her beneficial, steadying influence.

Student Writing Sample #1

> John Adams's marriage to Abigail was the most important choice in his life. He was to come to understand this better with time. In so many ways, she was his equal, and he could not have imagined the importance of the role she was going to play, despite his love for her and his appreciation of her good, solid influence.

UNACCEPTABLE! This paragraph is the work of someone either deliberately plagiarizing or someone who doesn't understand what it means to plagiarize. The writer may have changed a few words and switched the order of words in the sentences, but the writer has not changed McCullough's sequence of ideas and has not used the information in a meaningful way. He or she failed to cite what are really McCullough's original ideas or words.

Student Writing Sample #2

> When John Adams was ready to marry, he sought a woman who was his equal. He found Abigail Smith and loved her for her steadying influence.

UNACCEPTABLE! Not only did this student neglect to cite, but also this paraphrase twists McCullough's meaning. Though it changes words significantly, it does a poor job conveying the original idea accurately.

Student Writing Sample #3

> The best decisions of a great leader may extend beyond the political. In fact, the course of American history may have been changed by an entirely personal decision. In his biography of Adams, David McCullough notes that Adams's choice of Abigail Smith as a wife was the most critical decision of his life. "She was in all respects his equal and the part she was to play would be greater than he could possibly have imagined" (57).

ACCEPTABLE! The author uses the information in a meaningful way, accurately paraphrases the ideas presented in the original source, credits them, and weaves in a quotation to emphasize the point. The source is properly quoted and cited using quotation marks and in-text documentation. Because the source is noted in the text, only the page number appears in parentheses. Note that in this example the student created his or her own topic sentence, following an independent plan and not necessarily following the structure of another author's material.

You Can Avoid Plagiarism

- When you take notes, make sure that you copy all original passages in quotation marks.
- Paraphrase by putting ideas into your own words; go beyond changing a few words. Recognize that paraphrasing of unique ideas and facts also requires citation.
- As you write, return to the text and check your paraphrase against the original source to make sure you haven't unintentionally copied.
- Use graphic organizers to restructure your facts and ideas.
- Use your own voice to put a new twist on old information.
- When in doubt, cite!

What Is "Common Knowledge"?

You don't have to cite everything. Facts or ideas referred to as "common knowledge" do not have to be cited.

- Common knowledge includes facts that are found in many sources—facts that you assume many people know. A rule of thumb is that if you find a fact in three or more sources, it may be considered common knowledge. (As you research, make a check mark on your note cards each time you encounter a particular specific fact. When a note card has more than three check marks, you may assume that fact is common knowledge.)
- An example of common knowledge is that John Adams married Abigail Smith.
- Remember, you must document little-known facts and any ideas that interpret facts, even if they are paraphrased! For instance, even if you don't use McCullough's words, you should absolutely document McCullough's belief that Adams's marriage was the most critical decision of his life.

DOCUMENTING YOUR SOURCES

BOOK BY TWO OR MORE AUTHORS

Foulke, Robert, and Paul Smith. *An Anatomy of Literature*. New York: Harcourt, 1972.

BOOK THAT IS EDITED OR A CRITICAL EDITION

Dryden, John. *A Collection of Critical Essays*. Ed. Bernard N. Schilling. Englewood Cliffs: Prentice-Hall, 1963.

BOOK WITH A CORPORATE AUTHOR

Commission on the Arts. *The Arts in Spanish Life*. Madrid: U. of Madrid, 1980.

BOOK WITH NO AUTHOR'S NAME GIVEN

Webster's Biographical Dictionary. New York: Merriam, 1961.

BOOK, ANTHOLOGY

Chaucer, Geoffrey. "The Nun's Priest's Tale." *An Anthology of Famous English and American Poetry*. Ed. William Rose Benet and Conrad Aiken. New York: Random House, 1945.

BOOK, AN "EDITION"

Shakespeare, William. *Hamlet*. Ed. Louis B. Wright and Virginia A. LaMar. Folger Library ed. New York: Washington Square, 1958.

BOOK, TRANSLATION

Dostoevsky, Fyodor. *Crime and Punishment*. Trans. Constance Garnett. New York: Bantam, 1981.

CRITICAL ANALYSIS, SIGNED EXCERPT

Ross, Stephan S. "Tom Wolfe." *Contemporary Literary Criticism*. Ed. Daniel G. Marowski. 35: 458–60.

ENCYCLOPEDIA, SIGNED ARTICLE

Gerber, John C. "Naturalism." *World Book Encyclopedia*. 2003.

ENCYCLOPEDIA, UNSIGNED ARTICLE

"Tennyson, Alfred, Lord." *Encyclopaedia Britannica*. 2000.

ENCYCLOPEDIA ARTICLE ON CD-ROM

Author's Last Name, First Name (if signed). "Title of Article." *Title of Reference Work*. Edition or version (if available). City of Publication: Publisher, Year of Publication.

Ramet, Sabrina P. "Kosovo." *Encarta Deluxe 2002*. CD-ROM. Redmond, Wash.: Microsoft, 2000.

You may not be able to find all of the information for a CD-ROM citation. For example, the city of publication may be difficult to find. Simply cite whatever information is available.

ENCYCLOPEDIA WITH EDITOR/COMPILER

Benet, William Rose, ed. "Recessional." *Reader's Encyclopedia*. New York: Crowell, 1965.

FILM

The Picture of Dorian Gray. Dir. Albert Lewin. With George Sanders and Donna Reed. Metro-Goldwyn-Mayer, 1972.

INTERVIEW

Shields, N. T. Personal interview. 26 Mar. 1979.

MAGAZINE/PERIODICAL ARTICLE

Note: Titles of magazines and journals are *not* followed by periods.

From a Monthly Publication

Ramsey, Pamela. "Where's My Smiley Face?" *MacWorld* Sept. 1997: 86–94.

From a Weekly or Biweekly

Henry, Mary Ann. "Announcing Bus Changes with Flair." *Time* 4 July 1991: 17–76.

From a Journal with Continuous Pagination

Skater, Andrew. "Rollerblading on a Secondary Level." *Secondary Education* 54 (2001): 113–25.

PAMPHLET, SIGNED

Bush, Gail. "The Principal's Manual for Your School Library Media Program." Chicago: American Association of School Librarians, 2000.

PAMPHLET, UNSIGNED

Follett Library Book Co. *Follett Forum.* Crystal Lake: Follett, Feb. 1988.

PERIODICAL ARTICLE ON CD-ROM

Nethead, Jane. "Email Rules." *New York Times* 15 Nov. 1995, late ed.: B3. *New York Times Ondisc.* CD-ROM. UMI-ProQuest. Jan. 1996.

PERSONAL LETTER, UNPUBLISHED

Steinbeck, John. Letter to Princess Grace of Monaco. 6 Nov. 1962.

RADIO OR TELEVISION PROGRAM

The Last Voyage. Narr. Jacques Cousteau. Writ. and prod. Jacques Cousteau. PBS Special. WHYY, Philadelphia. 17 Jan. 1972.

REFERENCE SERIES, UNSIGNED

Moritz, Charles, ed. "Potok, Chaim." *Current Biography Yearbook 1983.* 307–11.

REVIEW

Hughes, Riley. "Salinger, Jerome David." *Book Review Digest 1951.* Ed. Mertia M. James and Dorothy Brown. 772.

VIDEOTAPE

The North Star. Videocassette. Dir. Bruce Goddard. PBS Video, 1984. 50 min.

CITING ONLINE SOURCES

Not all web pages will have all the information recommended for inclusion in citations. If you've looked carefully and a required piece of information is not available, simply leave it out. In documenting online resources, it is most important to give the reader as much essential information as possible (e.g., author, title, publication date, URL) to identify the source you are citing.

Remember to check a current copy of the *MLA Handbook for Writers of Research Papers* for further information and more examples.

What about In-Text Citations?

For traditional print sources, in-text citations include the author's name and the page(s) cited. Because electronic documents rarely contain page numbers, in most instances your in-text citation will include only the author's name—for example, (Smith). If your electronic document has no author, use the title of the page. You may use a shortened version of the title as long as it is distinct—for example, ("Cloning"). If paragraphs in an electronic document are numbered, include that information—for example, (Smith pars. 112–20). Do not cite page numbers from your printouts; pagination varies with different printers and fonts.

URLs from Databases: What about Those Long URLs?

When working with articles from online databases (like EBSCOhost, GaleNet, or bigchalk), it is likely that an article's URL will be quite long. These URLs may not be "durable." That is, they may not be permanently attached to the article and would not be particularly useful in identifying and relocating it. When working with long URLs from databases, it is acceptable to truncate after the first slash mark, as long as the address of the database you used is clearly noted. Do *not* include names of browsers (Netscape, Microsoft Explorer) or search tools (Yahoo!, AltaVista, Ask Jeeves) in your citations.

Formatting Your Citations

World Wide Web (General Website)

Author (if known). "Title of Page or Document." *Title of site or larger work* (if applicable). Name of editor, compiler, or translator (if any). Publication information for any print version of the source. Date of electronic publication, last update, or date of posting. Name of any associated institution. Date of download. <http://addressofsite>.

Deville, Carol. "Social Studies Research and the Web." *SocialStudiesWorld.net.* 8 June 2001. Social Studies Consortium. 3 Oct. 2001. <http://www.socstudworld.net/research.htm>.

Smith, George. "Graf Has Look of a Champion." *ESPNET SportsZone.* 29 Aug. 1996. 5 May 1999. <http://www.espn.com/gen/top/0108716001.html>.

Reprints: Much of the material you access from online databases has been previously published, either in print or electronically. In these cases, you will be citing the original publication information, followed by information relating to the online database, followed by information related to the online service hosting that database.

Magazine Article Accessed on the Web (Not through a Subscription Database)

Author. "Title of Article." *Title of Magazine* Date of electronic publication. Date of access. <http://addressofpage>.

Smith, Jane. "Who Really Invented the Internet?" *Web Weekly* 26 Feb. 2001. 4 May 2001. <http://webweekly.com/smithwho/>.

Article in an Online Reference Database or Encyclopedia

Author. "Title of Article." *Title of Reference Work.* Edition or version (if available). Date. *Title of Database or Online Service.* Date of access. <http://addressofdatabase>.

Cook, Sarah Gibbard. "Berlin, Germany." *Americana Online.* Vers. 99.1. Mar. 2002. *Encyclopedia Americana.* 29 Feb. 2003. <http://go.grolier.com>.

Journal Accessed through a Subscription Service (EBSCOhost, etc.)

Note: Periodical titles are *not* followed by a period.

Author. "Article Title." *Periodical Title* Date of print publication (if available): pages. *Database name* (if any). Publisher (if appropriate). Date of access. <http://addressofdatabase>.

Clark, Charles S. "The FBI under Fire." *CQ Researcher* 11 April 1997: 315–22. 3 Sept. 1999. <http://resource.cq.com>.

Brown, Charlie. "My Life in Cartoons." *Cartoon Week* 21 Nov. 2001: 7–12. *General Reference Center Gold.* Gale Group. 15 Dec. 2003. <http://www.galenet.com/>.

SIRS Online Products

Author. "Article Title." *Original Source of Article* Date of original source: pages. *Database name.* Date of access. <http://addressofdatabase>.

SIRS Researcher example:
Frick, Robert. "Investing in Medical Miracles." *Kiplinger's Personal Finance* Feb. 1999: 80–87. *SIRS Knowledge Source: Researcher.* [You may need to substitute *Renaissance* or *Government Reporter*] 25 July 2003. <http://sks.sirs.com/>.

FACTS.com

"Article Title." *Original Source of Article* Date of original source. *Database name.* Company name. Date of access. <http://addressofdatabase>.

"Safe Drinking Water Act Signed." *Facts On File World News Digest* 22 Aug. 1996. *FACTS.com.* Facts On File News Services. 20 Jan. 2000. <http://www.2facts.com>.

"Issues and Controversies: Racial Disparities." *Issues and Controversies On File* 13 Jan. 2002. *FACTS.*

com. Facts On File News Services. 28 Feb. 2002. <http://www.2facts.com>.

Gale Resource Centers

FORMAT FOR A PERIODICAL REFERENCE

Author. "Article Title." *Original Source of Article* Date of original source: Pages of original source. *Specific Database* on *Student Resource Center.* Gale Group. Date of access. <http://addressofdatabase>.

Feldman, Elaine. "Death by Chocolate: Facts and Myths." *Nutrition Today* 1 May 1998: 106–12. *Health Module* on *Student Resource Center.* Gale Group. 15 Dec. 2001. <http://www.galenet.com>.

FORMAT FOR AN ARTICLE THAT APPEARED IN A BOOK

Author. "Article Title." *Title of Book.* City of publication: Publisher, Date. Pages. *Specific Database* on *Larger Database.* Gale Group. Date of access. <http://www.galenet.com>.

Baker, Carlos. "Hemingway's Ancient Mariner." *Ernest Hemingway: Critiques of Four Major Novels.* Ed. Carlos Baker. New York: Scribners, 1962. 156–72. *Literature Resource Center.* Gale Group. 26 July 2003. http://www.galenet.com.

FORMAT FOR A REFERENCE ARTICLE

Author (if provided). "Article Title." *Specific Database* on *Student Resource Center Gold.* Gale Group. Date of access. <http://www.galenet.com>.

"Classical Greek Civilization, 2000 B.C.–300 B.C." *DISCovering World History* on *Student Resource Center Gold.* Gale Group. 12 Oct. 1999. <http://www.galenet.com>.

"Dean Koontz." *DISCovering Authors Modules* on *Student Resource Center.* Gale Group. 3 Dec. 2001. <http://galenet.gale.com>.

FORMAT FOR A REPUBLISHED JOURNAL ESSAY

Author (if provided). "Article Title." *Original Source of Article.* Date of original source: Pages of original source. *Specific Database* on *Larger Database.* Gale Group. Date of access. <http://www.galenet.com>.

Levin, Harry. "Wonderland Revisited." *The Kenyon Review* Autumn, 1965: 591–93. *Contemporary Literary Criticism* on *Student Resource Center Gold.* Gale Group. 20 Oct. 2002. <http://galenet.gale.com>.

Citing Online Sources (Continued)

FORMAT FOR A REPUBLISHED JOURNAL ESSAY (Continued)

Berger, Carol. "Profile of a Basketball Great." *Sports in Philadelphia* 12 Nov. 1999: 23–24. *Biography Resource Center*. Gale Group. 20 Dec. 2003. <http://www.galenet.com>.

WilsonWeb Biography

"Edward Albee." *Current Biography 1996* 27 Oct. 1997. *Wilson Biographies Plus* on *WilsonWeb*. 15 Dec. 2002. <http://hwwilsonweb.com/>.

Electronic Mailing List

Author (if given). "Subject of Message." Date of posting. Online posting. Name of List. Date of access. <URL or email address of the list>.

Williams, Jim. "Computer to T.V. Screen." 6 Aug. 1995. Online posting. Global Technology Discussion Group. 21 Nov. 2001. <http://www.gtdg.org> or <listserv@citation.edu>.

Online Chat/Synchronous Communication

Name of Speaker (if available). "Description of the event." Date of session or event. Forum of the communication. Date of access. <web or network address>.

Yente, Ima. "Online discussion of future fuels." 24 Oct. 1997. EnvironMOO. 28 June 2002. <telnet://IRC@envirosite.edu>.

Email, Personal

Sender's Last Name, First Name. "Subject line from posting." Date of posting. Personal email (or Email to Recipient's Name). Date of access.

Smith, William. "Trial results." 12 Jan. 2001. Email to John Henry. 29 May 2002.

Online Chat

Name of Speaker (if available). Date of session. Online chat. <IRC address, IRC channel name, or URL>.

Yente, Ima. Online. 24 Oct. 1997. Online chat. <http://www.yenta.org>.

Online Image

Artist (if available). "Description or Title of Image." Date of image. Online image. *Title of Larger Site*. Date of access. <http://address.website.org>.

"Mars Landing." Online image. 3 Nov. 1999. *NASA Home Page.* <http://www.nasa.org>.

Weaver, Bruce. "Challenger Explosion." 28 Jan 1986. Online image. *AP Photo Archive*. 30 Jan. 2002. <http://accuweather.ap.org/cgi-bin/aplaunch.pl>.

Online Sound

Creator (if available). "Description or Title of Sound." Date of sound. Online sound. *Title of Larger Site*. Date of download. <http://addressofwebsite>.

"This Week's Saturday Radio Address." 25 Oct. 1998. Online sound. *Whitehouse Briefing Room*. 23 Oct. 2000. <http://www.whitehouse.gov/WH/html/briefroom.html>.

Online Video Clip

"Description or Title of Video Clip." Date of clip. Online video clip. *Title of Larger Site*. Date of download. <http://addressofwebsite>.

"Hindenburg Broadcast." 6 May 1937. Online video clip. *Encarta Online Deluxe*. 4 Nov. 2000. <http://encarta.msn.com/encarta/MediaMax.asp?z>.

But my word processor removes angle brackets < > whenever I hit "return." Does it matter? What should I do?

MLA Style (http://www.mla.org) notes that "hyperlinks may be useful for documents that are read on-screen. When a document is printed, however, the linking has no purpose. A research paper . . . should be free of the irrelevant effects of hyperlinks."

To get rid of those irrelevant links, you can enter "Control Z" (Undo AutoFormat) or, as the MLA suggests for recent versions of Word, "you can turn off automatic hyperlinking by going to the menu 'Tools' and choosing 'AutoCorrect.' Then click on the tab 'AutoFormat As You Type,' and remove the check mark next to 'Internet and network paths with hyperlinks.'"

WORKS CITED AND WORKS CONSULTED PAGES

What's the Difference?

Works Consulted is the term for the list of sources used in the preparation of a research project. This list includes background reading, summarized sources, or any sources used for informational purposes but not paraphrased or quoted. The list is used to document those sources referred to, but not cited, in your project.

Works Cited is the term for the list of sources actually documented (paraphrased or quoted) in your project, generally through parenthetical citation. All the parenthetical references in the paper or project should lead the reader to this list of sources.

When Should You Use Them?

- You might prepare only a Works Consulted page if you did not quote or paraphrase at all in the project.

- You might prepare only a Works Cited page if you paraphrased or quoted from, and therefore cited, all sources used.

- You might prepare *both* a Works Consulted and a Works Cited page if, in addition to the sources cited in the project or paper, you also consulted other sources that were not paraphrased or quoted.

How Should You Prepare the Works Cited and Works Consulted Pages?

- Head a new sheet of paper "Works Cited" or "Works Consulted." (Do not use quotation marks around your title.)

- Alphabetize your sources by author or by first entry, which may be an association or a title if no author is noted. This should be easy if you have collected source cards.

- Place the Works Cited page(s) immediately after the last page of the text.

- If your paper includes both Works Cited and Works Consulted, the Works Consulted page should follow the Works Cited page.

Developed with Carol H. Rohrbach, coordinator of language arts, School District of Springfield Township, Erdenheim, Pa.

SOURCE CARDS

Name _____

Source #

Magazine Article in an Online Database (Source Card)

Author(s) _____

Title of Article _____

Magazine _____

Date _____ Page #s _____

Database Name _____ Publisher_____

Date of Access _____

URL (shortened form) _____

Notes/Quotes _____

_____

Example: Author. "Article Title." *Periodical Title* Date of print publication (if available): pages. *Database Name* (if any). Publisher (if appropriate). Date of access. <http://addressofdatabase>.

- -

Name _____

Source #

Reference Article in an Online Database (Source Card)

Author(s) _____

Title of Article _____

Book Title/Original Source_____

City of Publication _____ Publisher _____ Date of Publication _____

Page #s _____

Database Name _____

Publisher _____

Date of Access _____

URL (shortened form) _____

Notes _____

_____

Example: Author (if available). "Article Title." *Specific Database/Reference Work* on *Larger Database*. Date. *Title of Database or Online Service*. Publisher. Date of access. <addressofdatabase>.

Name _____

General Website (Source Card)

Author(s) if Noted _____

Title of Page or Document _____

Title of Larger Site _____

Date of Electronic Publication/Last Update/Posting _____

Name of any Associated Institution _____

Date of Access _____

URL _____

Notes/Quotes _____

_____

Example: Author. "Title of Page." *Title of Larger Site.* Date of publication. Name of Associated Institution. Date of access. <http://addressofsite.>

Name _____

Source #

Online Image/Sound/Videoclip (Source Card)

Artist/Creator (if noted) _____

Description or Title of Media _____

Date Image/Sound/Clip Was Created _____

Online Image/Online Sound/Online Videoclip _____

Date of Electronic Publication/Last Update/Posting _____

Title of Larger Site _____

Date of Access _____

URL _____

Notes _____

_____

Example: Artist. "Description or title of media." Date created. Online image/sound/videoclip. *Title of Larger Site.* Date of access. <http://addressofsite>.

NOTE CARDS

Subtopic	Source #	Page(s) #

Notes/Quotes

Name _____ Class _____

Subtopic	Source #	Page(s) #

Notes/Quotes

Name _____ Class _____

QUOTING, PARAPHRASING, AND SUMMARIZING

You *can* borrow from the works of other writers as you research. Good writers use three strategies—quoting, paraphrasing, and summarizing—to blend source materials in with their own, while making sure their own voice is heard.

Quotations are the exact words of an author, copied directly from the source word for word. Quotations must be cited!
Use quotations when:

- You want to add the power of an author's words to support your argument
- You want to disagree with an author's argument
- You want to highlight particularly eloquent or powerful phrases or passages
- You are comparing and contrasting specific points of view
- You want to note the important research that precedes your own

Paraphrasing means rephrasing the words of an author, putting his or her thoughts in your own words. A paraphrase can be viewed as a "translation" of the original source. When you paraphrase, you rework the source's ideas, words, phrases, and sentence structures with your own. Paraphrased text is often, but not always, slightly shorter than the original work. Like quotations, paraphrased material must be followed with in-text documentation and cited on the Works Cited page.
Paraphrase when:

- You plan to use information on your note cards and wish to avoid plagiarizing
- You want to avoid overusing quotations
- You want to use your own voice to present information

Summarizing involves putting the main idea(s) of one or several writers into your own words, including only the main point(s). Once again, it is necessary to attribute summarized ideas to the original source. Summarized ideas are not necessarily presented in the same order as in the original source. Summaries are significantly shorter than the original and take a broad overview of the source material.
Summarize when:

- You want to establish background or offer an overview of a topic
- You want to describe common knowledge (from several sources) about a topic
- You want to determine the main ideas of a single source

Developed with Carol H. Rohrbach, coordinator of language arts, School District of Springfield Township, Erdenheim, Pa.

STUDENT GUIDELINES FOR MULTIMEDIA AND WEB PAGE PRODUCTION

Technology has dramatically changed the manner in which people share ideas and information. Students now have unprecedented access to information in all its forms—text, images, sound, and video. This new access, combined with the new ease with which people can publish electronically, has added to the complexity of copyright issues.

Our school district is concerned about teaching our students to behave responsibly in an electronic environment, and we expect students to respect the integrity of intellectual property.

The following are guidelines to aid you in creating research products using technology. They summarize the *Fair Use Guidelines for Educational Multimedia* (http://www.libraries.psu.edu/mtss/fairuse/guidelinedoc.html) produced by the Consortium of College and University Media Centers in 1996.

In creating academic multimedia products, using such products as KidPix, HyperStudio, or PowerPoint, students may use the "lawfully acquired copyrighted" works of others with proper credit and citations. You may perform and display your own educational multimedia projects in the course for which they were created. You may also retain them as examples of your academic work for later personal uses, such as job and graduate school interviews.

The best strategy in creating multimedia projects is to "be conservative." Use only small amounts of the works of others and cite them carefully. Do not make any unnecessary copies—no more than two "use copies" and one additional backup copy. (If a group created the project, each major contributor may make his or her own copy, but only for the purpose for which the project was originally created.)

Crediting Sources

Include a note on the opening screen of your project stating that some materials in the presentation are included in accordance with the *Fair Use Guidelines for Multimedia* and are restricted from further use.

You should credit all sources of copyrighted information with full bibliographic citations, including author, title, publisher, and place and date of publication, URL, etc. This bibliographic information may be combined and shown in a separate section of the project. (There are exceptions for images when used for distance learn-ing.) Try to follow a format similar to in-text documentation for a print product. Include a small note under an image or a piece of text that corresponds to your Works Cited slide. If the copyright notice © and copyright ownership information are shown in the original source, you must show it in your credits.

If there is a possibility that you will later use your multimedia project in another way, for example, dissemination on the Web, you should take steps to obtain permission to use all copyrighted portions while the project is being developed rather than waiting until the project is completed.

Portions Used

Specific guidelines limit the portions of copyrighted works students are allowed to use in a multimedia project. Portion use varies according to information format.

TEXT

- Up to 10 percent or 1,000 words, whichever is less, of a copyrighted work

POEMS

- The entire poem if less than 250 words; 250 words or less if using a longer poem
- No more than 5 poems (or excerpts) by different poets, from an anthology
- No more than 3 poems (or excerpts) by one poet

MUSIC OR LYRICS

- Up to 10 percent of a copyrighted musical composition, but no more than 30 seconds from an individual musical work
- Any alterations cannot change the basic melody or the fundamental character of the work.

ILLUSTRATIONS

- A photograph or illustration may be used in its entirety.
- No more than 5 images by an artist or a photographer
- No more than 10 percent or no more than 15 images from a collection

MOTION MEDIA

- Up to 10 percent of a copyrighted work or 3 minutes, whichever is less

NUMERICAL DATA SETS

- Up to 10 percent or 2,500 fields or cell entries, whichever is less, from a copyrighted database or data table

Internet Use in Multimedia Presentations

Care should be taken in downloading material from Internet sites for use in multimedia presentations. Be aware that some copyrighted works have been posted to the Web without the authorization of the copyright holder.

Integrity of the Copyrighted Work: Alterations

Educators and students may make alterations in the portions of the copyrighted works used in an academic multimedia project only if the alterations support specific instructional objectives. All alterations must be noted.

Permission Is Required

- for multimedia projects used for noneducational or commercial purposes
- for duplication or distribution of multimedia projects beyond limitations outlined above (posting on the Web, for example)
- when distributing the project over an electronic network

Publishing on the Web

The *Fair Use Guidelines for Multimedia* do not extend to web publishing. They end when the creator of the multimedia project loses control of his or her product's use, such as when others access it over the Internet. Students should take steps to obtain permission for all copyrighted portions of a web product, unless it is clearly noted that these materials are in the public domain and are available for free use. Requests for permission should begin while the project is being developed.

Requesting Permission of a Copyright Holder

When writing for permission, you are more likely to get a positive response if you:

- make it easy for the copyright holder or creator to respond
- are very clear and specific about what material(s) you want to use
- are very clear on how you plan to use the material(s)
- make your request politely and intelligently

Remember:

- Ask only for what you really need.
- Write early so that you have a better chance of getting a response before your deadline.
- If you are sending a request via regular mail, include a stamped, self-addressed envelope.

PERMISSION LETTER TEMPLATE

The following is a template for a letter you might mail or email requesting permission to use copyrighted work in your multimedia projects. You need permission, not merely documentation, if you plan to include copyrighted media in a broadcast show or a web publication. Import this letter into a word-processing program and edit it carefully before emailing it.

Date
Publisher's Name (if available)
Publisher's Address (if available)

Dear Sir or Madam (substitute name if known),

I am a student at _____, and I am writing to ask permission to use _____ [a quote or picture or music or video clip—be specific about exactly what piece of copyrighted material you are asking for] in my web project/television broadcast. This project is a school assignment for my _____ class. I expect the project to be posted on our school's website/running on the cable network on _____ [date/s].

Thank you for considering my request. If you agree, I will properly cite the source. Please let me know if you'd like me to follow any special instructions for acknowledging this material.

Sincerely,
Your name
School
School Address
http://www.springfield.k12.pa.us
email

* *

Permission granted (signature, if sent through regular mail)

_____

Full name _____

Title_____

Date _____

Conditions/Instructions (if any) _____

_____

WEAVING QUOTES INTO YOUR WRITING

Effective writers use a variety of techniques to integrate quotations into their text. When you use a quote in your writing, consider:

- What am I trying to say?
- Can a passage from the text say it for me?
- Have I explained the value of the quote?

Avoid "overquoting." It is important that your own voice is heard!

Discuss the effectiveness of the following writing samples.

Serious room for improvement

William Golding's book *Lord of the Flies* is about kids stranded on an island. Some of the kids are good and some are bad. "Roger, with a sense of delirious abandonment, leaned all his weight on the lever" (Golding 180). So I ask you, what causes irresponsible behavior? Ralph is good, but Jack is bad.

Room for improvement

There are bad kids on the island. One of them is Roger. He drops a boulder on Piggy and kills him. "Roger, with a sense of delirious abandonment, leaned all his weight on the lever" (Golding 180). This caused Piggy's death.

A possible revision

The truest form of wickedness on the island is evident in Roger. He demonstrates his true depravity when, "with a sense of delirious abandonment, [he] leaned all his weight on the lever" (Golding 180). Well aware of Piggy's place beneath him, Roger willingly takes Piggy's life.

Another possible revision

Roger's murder of Piggy clearly illustrates the depths children can sink to without appropriate supervision. As he stood high above Piggy on the mountain, "Roger, with a sense of delirious abandonment, leaned all his weight on the lever" (Golding 180). His willingness to welcome the moment with "delirious abandonment" clearly demonstrates the level of pleasure that Roger received by committing this horrific act.

By Ken Rodoff, English teacher, Springfield Township High School, Erdenheim, Pa. Adapted by Joyce Valenza.

3

Evaluation

From *Information Power*

Information Literacy

Standard 2: The student who is information literate evaluates information critically and competently.

Indicators

1. Determines accuracy, relevance, and comprehensiveness
2. Distinguishes among fact, point of view, and opinion
3. Identifies inaccurate and misleading information
4. Selects information appropriate to the problem or question at hand

From *NETS for Students*

Standard 5: Technology Research Tools

- Students use technology to locate, evaluate, and collect information from a variety of sources.
- Students evaluate and select new information resources and technological innovations based on the appropriateness for specific tasks.

From *Information Literacy Competency Standards for Higher Education* (Association of College and Research Libraries)

Standard 3: The information literate student evaluates information and its sources critically and incorporates selected information into his or her knowledge base and value system.

Performance Indicators

2. The information literate student articulates and applies initial criteria for evaluating both the information and its sources.

4. The information literate student compares new knowledge with prior knowledge to determine the value added, contradictions, or other unique characteristics of the information.

5. The information literate student determines whether the new knowledge has an impact on the individual's value system and takes steps to reconcile differences.

6. The information literate student validates understanding and interpretation of the information through discourse with other individuals, subject-area experts, and/or practitioners.

RELATED POSTERS

Evaluating Web Resources
URLs: Clues to Content

Evaluation is a tough skill to transmit. As adults, we have a broad scope of knowledge that may allow us to instantly recognize the name of a reputable organization like the American Cancer Society, or a prominent figure in a specific professional arena. Students, however, have no such scope. They have little background for determining quality. B.W. (Before the Web) students had help selecting information. Publishers, book and journal editors, booksellers, and librarians carefully filtered their research fodder for reliability and quality. But, alas, the Web is a self-publishing medium. In the unchecked landscape of the Web, it is especially important for students to be discerning consumers of information. The job of assessing accuracy, relevance, validity, bias, and datedness now falls into their laps. This job requires of them a good deal of judgment. Although the Web allows a truly democratic voice to all who care to contribute, noise and garbage are insidious by-products of its glorious democracy. And today's students are really the first generation to cope with true information overload and true information diversity.

The fact is that our students may be developmentally unprepared to cope with the level of evaluation expected of them. We need to offer them every possible opportunity to practice, and we need to guide students as they

- evaluate their search tools
- evaluate their results lists
- evaluate authors' credentials
- holistically evaluate the sites they plan to use in the context of their information needs
- evaluate their own work, including the research process

It is no real revelation that our students are heavily reliant on web-based materials. For many, the Web is the *only* source. We need to convey that not all information is created equal and that evaluation, combined with a healthy dose of skepticism, is an essential strategy students will need to carry with them throughout the research process—indeed, throughout their lives.

It's not all cognitive. A major issue in effective evaluation is motivation. Because it is easy for students to locate some information on the Web, they may not necessarily be motivated to look harder for the *best* information. It is up to us as teachers and librarians to instill that desire, to design opportunities in which we require students to practice evaluation, and to hold them accountable for finding "the right stuff."

The activities in this chapter model the type of selection students would go through in accepting or rejecting information for a research product. In addition, these activities address how to evaluate the research process as a whole. Most can be adapted for various ability levels.

ACTIVITIES AND HANDOUTS

Evaluation: CARRDSS: Though students may have a bit of trouble remembering which letters are doubled, CARRDSS (see p. 65) works as a schoolwide acronym to remind students of the criteria they must consider in evaluating their sources.

Why Should I Take This Author Seriously? This handout (see p. 66), created for upper-level high-school students, should help them assess the qualifications of a web page (or any other) author. Because credentials are often hidden on web pages, students benefit from a discussion of the detective work they might employ to discover who an author really is.

Ask Yourself Questions: This material (see p. 68) could be used as a handout or displayed during an initial class discussion of evaluating web pages.

Thinking about Your Research: Essential Questions to Assure an "A" Project!: Use this chart (see p. 69) to introduce the habits and behaviors displayed by thoughtful, effective researchers through the various steps of the research process.

Research CheckBric: This assessment tool, developed in collaboration with Language Arts Coordinator Carol Rohrbach, focuses on the research process, analyzes the criteria valuable in scholarly research, and communicates clearly to students the steps they should follow to create a successful product. The tool (see p. 70) assumes that students submit a research package that includes a reflection and a search organizer. "Quotable quotes" are quotations truly *worth* quoting, quotations that further the student writer's narrative. "Research holes" are the major sources that students might overlook.

Research Project Rubric: This rubric (see p. 72) ensures students cover all the steps in the research process.

Multimedia Project/Web Page Evaluation Rubric: The allure of multimedia may lead students to believe that they can put less thought into their PowerPoints and web pages than into their formal research papers. This rubric (see p. 73) values research, organization, presentation, and documentation, as well as multimedia style.

Web-Based Pathfinder Rubric: This rubric (see p. 76) will help assess the Pathfinder project described in the chapter on organizing and communicating.

Position Paper and *Thesis Oral Defense Rubrics:* These two rubrics (see pp. 79 and 80) work together. Students engaged in thesis-driven research are likely to be required to orally defend their positions. These rubrics were developed by Michael Wagman, teacher of the gifted, School District of Springfield Township.

Research Conference Form: Research is a process and as a process it should be evaluated and refined (see p. 81). If we examine only finished products, we often find ourselves faced with research disasters and we ignore important learning opportunities. Research conferences provide opportunities to guide students before they hit the disaster stage. They show students that we value the process as well as the product. They involve the expertise of the librarian and allow students valuable opportunities to consult with information professionals.

Checklist for Research: Use this tool (see p. 82) to help guide students to the best resources before they complete their projects. It offers an opportunity to see potential searching problems and make important suggestions.

Reflecting on the Research Process: This tool (see p. 84), developed with Language Arts Coordinator Carol Rohrbach, asks students to focus and reflect on their process. When students know up front they will be graded on the process as well as the product, they take the process more seriously. Reflection encourages the serious consideration that will improve students' future research.

Comparing Subscription Services and Search Tools (High School and Middle School versions): These exercises (see pp. 85 and 86) expose students to a variety of search tools and should lead them to seriously consider the value of subscription databases for reliable results. Edit the activity based on your own subscription services or the search tools you would like to introduce or highlight.

Practice Ranking Sources (High School and Middle School versions): These activities (see pp. 87 and 88) allow students to practice decision making in examining results lists. There are no perfect answers here, and readability may be an important issue in a variety of school environments. What is important is that students take a serious look at the value of resources and that they understand that we, as teachers, will also evaluate their choices carefully. Students need practice in distinguishing among primary, secondary, and tertiary sources and in determining the intended audience for a document.

For a more authentic experience, do a preliminary search in the area your students will be researching. Gather a variety of results from your searches in both search engines and subscription databases, and paste them into a word document. Make enough copies of this composite results page to distribute to small groups in the class. Laminate and cut up these sets of results. Have students work in groups to arrange each set of results in order of their value to the project you have assigned. Discuss the groups' decisions as a class.

Web Page Evaluation Worksheet: Joe Barker of the Teaching Library, University of California, Berkeley, developed this form (see p. 89) as an activity to help students thoroughly evaluate and compare the sites they visit. Barker's hints lead students to analyze the aim or intent of a page.

Annotated Works Cited: Asking students to annotate their sources raises the research bar. Annotations require students to use critical research and evaluation skills. Use these guidelines (see p. 91) as a starting point. You might ask students to use annotations only for free web resources, or you might ask them to annotate their best sources.

Evaluating Web Sources for Your Research Project: This organizer (see p. 92) helps students record potential web sources and evaluate them at the same time. You may choose to tell students they don't necessarily need to record their print and database sources on this form. These have already gone through filtering or evaluation processes.

A WebQuest about Evaluating Web Pages: This adaptable, web-based activity (see p. 93), designed for grades 6 through 12, asks students to evaluate a set of web pages on a focused topic. Students assume an area of expertise—content, authority/credibility, usability/design, or bias/purpose. For greater curricular relevance, the teacher may choose to substitute any group of websites around the topic currently being studied.

Organizer for Evaluating Websites WebQuest: Distribute this organizer (see p. 94) to each student to help them with their evaluations.

EVALUATION: CARRDSS

C REDIBILITY: Who is the author? What are his or her credentials?

A CCURACY: Can facts, statistics, or other information be verified through other sources? Based on my knowledge, does the information seem accurate?

R ELIABILITY: Does the source present a particular view or bias?

R ELEVANCE: Does this information directly support my hypothesis/thesis or help to answer my question?

D ATE: When was this information created? When was it revised? Are these dates meaningful in terms of the subject matter?

S OURCES BEHIND THE TEXT: Did the author use reliable, credible sources?

S COPE: Does this source address my hypothesis/thesis/question in a comprehensive or peripheral way? Is it a scholarly or popular treatment?

Developed in collaboration with Carol H. Rohrbach, language arts coordinator, School District of Springfield Township, Erdenheim, Pa.

Who is she?

WHY SHOULD I TAKE THIS AUTHOR SERIOUSLY?

Have you heard the old saying, "garbage in, garbage out"?

As students, you are information consumers. You want to be sure the sources you use are credible.

If you are unsure of an author's credentials, you might have difficulty defending use of his or her work in your documentation. Your teacher is likely to question you if you quote an *expert* who is unknown. Do a little legwork before you complete your project. Think carefully before you include a source in your bibliography.

To verify an author's credentials:

- Search the Web for the author's resume or C.V. (curriculum vitae). A C.V. is a more formal, usually lengthier resume format, written by people in academic, research, or scientific environments. C.V.s generally include lists of publications, presentations, professional activities, and honors.

- Search biographical reference tools—for instance, *Wilson's Biographies* or Gale's *Biography Resource Center*. Gale's *Contemporary Authors*—in print or online— is extremely comprehensive and covers writers in all fields of knowledge from antiquity to modern day. Phone your nearest large public library and ask the reference librarian to check the *Who's Who* reference books in the appropriate subject area.

- Search for news of the author in a periodical database. Try using the author's name as a keyword in sources like EBSCOhost, Gale's *Student Resource Center,* or bigchalk.

- Do a "link check." In either AltaVista or Google, perform the following search: <link:yoururl>. Your results will show who else has linked to the page you are evaluating. Would the pages that link to your page be considered reputable? Do they review or annotate the page you are examining?

- Check to see if your page appears in a selective subject directory. For instance, has the page been included in the Librarians' Index to the Internet?

- Truncate the URL, if no affiliation is available on the page you are examining. Your goal is to try to get to the "root" page that might contain information "about this site."

Evaluate the author's credentials in these areas:

Education

- Does the person have an advanced degree? Is the degree related to the page you are evaluating? A professor of physics may not have particular expertise writing about the Holocaust.

- What evidence is offered of his or her knowledge? Be suspicious if the page lists no educational credentials. Are the letters after his or her name impressive? Ph.D.? Ed.D.?

- Is there evidence that the author is involved in significant research? Are there other studies by this author on the Web or in print?

- How well documented is the work the author is presenting?

- Be skeptical. Remember, everyone has a bias.

Experience

- How many years has the author been writing, teaching, studying, or researching?

- How active has the author been in his or her area of specialty? Have others mentioned or cited this author? (You might find this information in a web search.)

- Can you find other respected or scholarly publications this author has written?

- Does the author offer any firsthand, primary source–type experiences? A soldier present during the D-Day invasion would not have to have a university degree to offer important perspective on that event!

- Is the person active in the area of study? If you are researching the Olympic Games, a page written by a noted gymnast, runner, boxer, or skater might have great value.

- Be skeptical. Remember, everyone has a bias.

Affiliation/Reputation

- What is the author's institutional or business affiliation? What title does he or she hold?

- Is the page sponsored by an organization?

- Is the person involved with a university? Is it one you have heard of? Does it matter if he or she is involved with a major university or a community college?

- Is this person well known?

- In what types of journals is this author's work published? Popular? Scholarly/peer reviewed? Trade?

- What do others say about this author? Has his or her work been reviewed or criticized?

- Is the author's involvement commercial? Someone representing Philip Morris might approach the issue of smokers' rights in a way quite different from that of a representative of the American Cancer Society.

- Be skeptical. Remember, everyone has a bias.

ASK YOURSELF QUESTIONS

As you evaluate the information you find on the Web and consider it for use in your projects, ask yourself:

Affiliation/Bias/Purpose

Is the page associated with an institution, a company, a university, a government agency, or other organization?
Have I ever heard of the organization? Is it well respected?
Does the author's affiliation with the organization appear to bias the information?
Who is the intended audience? What is the purpose of this web page? Can I defend this source to my teacher?

Source

Who is the author?
What are his or her credentials?
Do I feel he or she is qualified to write on this topic?
Is he or she the creator of the information? (If not, what are his or her sources?) Can I defend this source to my teacher?

Content

Does the information appear to be accurate?
Is it verifiable?
Is it truly relevant to my needs? Can I defend this source to my teacher?

Currency

When was the information on this page created?
When was it last updated?
Are my information needs time-sensitive? Can I defend this source to my teacher?

THINKING ABOUT YOUR RESEARCH:
ESSENTIAL QUESTIONS TO ASSURE AN "A" PROJECT!

Defining Your Problem and Asking the Good Questions

- What is my thesis or problem? Is it focused enough to address in this project? Does it really interest me?
- What information do I need?
- What do I already know?
- What do I wonder about?
- Are there supporting questions I need to ask to better explore my topic?
- What more do I need to find out?

Remember: Try to make the most out of any research problem. The better your question, the more you will learn.

Accessing Information

- Where can I find the information I need?
- Which are the best possible sources?
- Which databases are the best choices? Should I search by keyword or topic?
- How can I search these sources effectively? Have I identified the best possible keywords and phrases to search or topics to browse?
- After reading, can I identify better keywords or subject headings to refine my electronic search?
- On the Web, should I begin with a search engine or a subject directory?
- What search strategies work best in the databases and web search tools I have chosen? (Boolean, phrase searching, field searching, etc.)
- Are there databases on the "invisible Web" that I should identify?
- Which types of sources will best address my problem? Do I need primary sources, journal articles, maps, etc.?
- Which sources do I already have?
- Would people help me in my search? Experts? Teachers? Librarians?
- Do I need help to find the resources I need or to make sure I haven't overlooked any critical sources?

Selecting and Evaluating Resources

- Do the resources I found really answer my questions or offer evidence to support my thesis?
- Have I carefully examined my selected sources for significant details and concepts?
- Have I examined my sources for currency, relevance, accuracy, credibility, appropriateness, and bias?
- Can I defend all of the resources I am considering for inclusion in my Works Cited or Works Consulted pages?
- Does the scope, depth, and quality of my research meet my teacher's and my own expectations?
- Which sources present the most compelling evidence?
- How will I credit my sources?

Organizing and Restructuring Information

- How much of the information I collected is truly relevant?
- Do I have a strategy for note taking?
- Do I see any patterns emerging in the information I collected?
- Should I construct a visual tool or written outline to help me structure my work?
- How can I organize this information so that it makes sense to others and myself?
- Have I solved my information problem and answered the related questions?
- Do I need additional information?

Communicating the Results of Your Research

- Who is my audience?
- How can I most effectively share this information with this audience?
- Which would be the best format for communicating the results of my information? PowerPoint? Video? Essay? Speech? Traditional paper? Other?
- What do I need to make this presentation? Equipment? Software?
- Have I included everything I want to share?
- Have I proofread, edited, and truly finished my project?

Evaluating Your Work

The product:
- Am I proud of my finished product?
- Was it effectively presented?
- Did I meet the guidelines or follow the rubric for the project?
- Am I sure I did not plagiarize from any of my sources?
- Is this the best work I could have done?

The process:
- Did I search electronic resources (the Web and licensed databases) effectively? Efficiently? Strategically?
- Did I explore the full scope of available resources and select the best?
- Did I approach the research process creatively and energetically?

RESEARCH CHECKBRIC

PLANNING   5   4   3   2   1   0

_____ Researcher(s) formulated a thoughtful hypothesis, question, or tentative thesis.

Thesis:

   _____ question/hypothesis or thesis prompted a meaningful "how" or "why" exploration

   _____ question/hypothesis or thesis focused

   _____ question/hypothesis or thesis did not lend itself to readily available answers

Comments:

GATHERING   5   4   3   2   1   0

_____ Researcher(s) gathered information from a full range of quality electronic and print sources, including appropriate subscription databases and primary sources.

   _____ used effective search strategies for locating information

      _____ brainstormed keywords, subject categories, related terms

      _____ used appropriate syntax for search tools

      _____ used appropriate search tools

   _____ evaluated resources (sources defendable according to CARRDSS)

   _____ consulted balanced resources (print, journals, websites)

   _____ used structured format(s) for extracting information from sources

Comments:

ORGANIZING   5   4   3   2   1   0

_____ Researcher(s) processed and synthesized ideas and information from various sources to answer question or prove thesis.

   _____ avoided "research holes" (All important sources are included.)

   _____ paraphrased effectively

   _____ used "quotable" quotations (quotations truly worthy of quoting)

   _____ integrated researcher's own ideas with quoted and paraphrased material

   _____ synthesized information to convey new understanding (researcher's voice)

   _____ used effective supporting evidence

   _____ used structuring tools (graphic organizers, outlines)

Comments:

Developed in collaboration with Carol H. Rohrbach, language arts coordinator, School District of Springfield Township, Erdenheim, Pa.

DOCUMENTING   5   4   3   2   1   0

_____ Researcher(s) used information ethically.

_____ credited ideas, text, graphics, media

_____ followed in-text documentation format correctly

_____ followed Works Cited/Works Consulted format correctly

Comments:

REFLECTING   5   4   3   2   1   0

_____ Researcher(s) reflected thoughtfully and specifically on the process.

Comments:

RESEARCH PROJECT RUBRIC

Student Name(s) _____ Teacher _____ Class _____ Final Grade _____

	Thesis/Problem/ Question	Information Seeking/Selecting and Evaluating	Analysis	Synthesis	Documentation	Product/Process
4	Student(s) posed a thoughtful, creative question that engaged them in challenging or provocative research. The question breaks new ground or contributes to knowledge in a focused, specific area.	Student(s) gathered information from a variety of quality electronic and print sources, including appropriate licensed databases. Sources are relevant and balanced, and include key readings relating to the thesis or problem. Primary sources were included (if appropriate).	Student(s) carefully analyzed the information collected and drew logical and inventive conclusions supported by evidence. Voice of the student writer is evident.	Student(s) developed appropriate structure for communicating the product, incorporating a variety of quality sources. Information is logically and creatively organized with smooth transitions.	Student(s) documented all sources, including visuals, sounds, and animations. Sources are properly cited, both in text/in-product and on Works Cited/Works Consulted pages/slides. Documentation is error-free.	Student(s) effectively and creatively used appropriate communication tools to convey their conclusions and demonstrated thorough, effective research techniques. Product displays creativity and originality.
3	Student(s) posed a focused question involving them in challenging research.	Student(s) gathered information from a variety of relevant sources—print and electronic.	Student(s)' product shows good effort was made in analyzing the evidence collected. Student writer's voice is heard.	Student(s) logically organized the product and made good connections among ideas.	Student(s) documented sources with some care. Sources are cited, both in-text/in-product and on Works Cited/Works Consulted pages/slides. Work includes few errors.	Student(s) effectively communicated the results of research to the audience.
2	Student(s) constructed a "so what" or "who cares" question that lends itself to readily available answers.	Student(s) gathered information from a limited range of sources and displayed minimal effort in selecting quality resources. Research has "holes."	Student(s)' conclusions could be supported by stronger evidence. Level of analysis could have been deeper. Where is the student writer's voice?	Student(s) could have put greater effort into organizing the product.	Student(s) need to use greater care in documenting sources. Documentation was poorly constructed or absent.	Student(s) need to work on communicating more effectively.
1	Student(s) developed a question requiring little creative thought.	Student(s) gathered information that lacked relevance, quality, depth, and balance. Research has significant "holes."	Student(s)' conclusions involved simply restating information. Conclusions not supported by evidence. Where is the student writer's voice?	Student(s)' work is not logically or effectively structured. No transitions were made among ideas.	Student(s) clearly plagiarized materials.	Student(s) showed little evidence of thoughtful research. Product does not effectively communicate research findings.
Teacher/ Librarian Comments	Points:	Points:	Points:	Points:	Points:	Points:

72

MULTIMEDIA PROJECT/WEB PAGE EVALUATION RUBRIC

Student(s) _____ Class _____ Date _____ Final Grade _____

	Assessment ___ Self ___ Peer ___ Teacher	Weight of Criteria (x 1, 2, 3)
	Scale	*Score*
MECHANICAL/TECHNICAL		
Project or page runs smoothly. Images load quickly. Student checked for all possible technical bugs.	5　　4　　3　　2　　1　　0 *Comments:*	
Navigation is intuitive and logical for content. All buttons and hyperlinks work effectively. Titles, subtitles, and sections are meaningful.	5　　4　　3　　2　　1　　0 *Comments:*	
Grammar, spelling, and punctuation are correct.	5　　4　　3　　2　　1　　0 *Comments:*	
All technical requirements set by the teacher are met or exceeded.	5　　4　　3　　2　　1　　0 *Comments:*	
APPEARANCE/CREATIVITY		
Screens or pages display elements of effective design. Choices of fonts, colors, and backgrounds are effective, tasteful, consistent. Text and media are artistically balanced, appropriately sized, and consistent with message.	5　　4　　3　　2　　1　　0 *Comments:*	
All media carefully selected to enhance message, support thesis, convey meaning.	5　　4　　3　　2　　1　　0 *Comments:*	
Project visually communicates student creativity. Student(s) used original art.	5　　4　　3　　2　　1　　0 *Comments:*	
		(Continued)

	Scale	Score
ORGANIZATION AND PRESENTATION OF CONTENT		
Information is presented in logical sequence or structure. Project demonstrates evidence of use of an organizer or note-taking strategy.	5 4 3 2 1 0 *Comments:*	
Project uses media to effectively structure information. Branching/hyperlinking of sections work to communicate information effectively.	5 4 3 2 1 0 *Comments:*	
Textual content is clearly and effectively written.	5 4 3 2 1 0 *Comments:*	
The work of others is effectively and selectively paraphrased, summarized, or quoted.	5 4 3 2 1 0 *Comments:*	
EVIDENCE OF QUALITY RESEARCH		
Student(s) developed a question or thesis worthy of research.	5 4 3 2 1 0 *Comments:*	
No "research holes." The most important sources were consulted.	5 4 3 2 1 0 *Comments:*	
Sources were critically evaluated. Student(s) used a full range of quality electronic and print sources, including appropriate databases and primary sources. Student(s) consulted resources that showed a variety of perspectives.	5 4 3 2 1 0 *Comments:*	
Student(s) displayed original thought in analyzing material from a variety of sources, drawing conclusions, and displaying deep understanding. Project is not merely a rehash of data; student voice is heard.	5 4 3 2 1 0 *Comments:*	

	Scale	Score
DOCUMENTATION		
All ideas, text, and media are properly cited following MLA style.	5 4 3 2 1 0 *Comments:*	
For web project or media broadcast, all permissions to use text, graphics, audio, and video, not in the public domain, are obtained and clearly noted.	5 4 3 2 1 0 *Comments:*	
GROUP WORK (IF COLLABORATIVE)		
Group members collaborated effectively. Each assumed appropriate roles and contributed in significant ways.	5 4 3 2 1 0 *Comments:*	
ORAL PRESENTATION (IF PRESENTED)		
Student(s) used effective presentation strategies—opening clincher, strong closing.	5 4 3 2 1 0 *Comments:*	
Students monitored audience for reaction, maintained eye contact, and projected voices to be clearly heard.	5 4 3 2 1 0 *Comments:*	
Presentation displayed evidence of rehearsal. Language was appropriate. Delivery was smooth.	5 4 3 2 1 0 *Comments:*	
Additional Project-Specific Criteria	5 4 3 2 1 0 *Comments:*	
Overall Comments		

WEB-BASED PATHFINDER RUBRIC

CONTENT						
Selected topic is focused, is of interest to others, and will help guide future researchers. *Comments:*	5	4	3	2	1	0
Introduction is clearly written and defines the scope and importance of the project. *Comments:*	5	4	3	2	1	0
Selected materials are consistently of high quality and display thoughtful evaluation. *Comments:*	5	4	3	2	1	0
Sources are comprehensive for the area of study. *Comments:*	5	4	3	2	1	0
Sources are balanced in terms of format and point of view. *Comments:*	5	4	3	2	1	0
Annotations are clearly written and convey the value of the source. *Comments:*	5	4	3	2	1	0

Student(s) identified scholars or experts in the field.	5	4	3	2	1	0
Comments:						

Web sources are evaluated and of consistent high quality.	5	4	3	2	1	0
Comments:						

There are no glaring "research holes." No critical work is missing.	5	4	3	2	1	0
Comments:						

Advice to future researchers is solid and useful.	5	4	3	2	1	0
Comments:						

APPEARANCE

Interface is clear, easy to read, and printer-friendly.	5	4	3	2	1	0
Comments:						

Sources are divided into logical categories.	5	4	3	2	1	0
Comments:						

(Continued)

Navigation bar is present if the page requires a lot of scrolling.	5	4	3	2	1	0
Comments:						
Format and graphic elements are consistent and enhance the message of the page.	5	4	3	2	1	0
Comments:						
Book titles, hyperlinks, and other formats are differentiated.	5	4	3	2	1	0
Comments:						
Page is spell-checked and grammatically correct.	5	4	3	2	1	0
Comments:						
Needs of the audience are considered and addressed through the design.	5	4	3	2	1	0
Comments:						
Teacher's Overall Comments:						
Librarian's Overall Comments:						
Grade:						

POSITION PAPER AND THESIS ORAL DEFENSE RUBRICS

(**Y** = Achieved, **N** = Needs Improvement)

Teacher	Position Paper	Student
	Thesis statement clearly defines position	
	Offers historical background to further understanding of the issue	
	Explains the controversy surrounding the issue	
	Summarizes the various existing points of view	
	Position is well supported by evidence showing how recognized experts or current studies support position	
	Discusses implications and recommends a course of action (if appropriate)	
	Conclusion is strong and persuasive	
	Paper is well documented with high-quality sources	
	Information is presented in the proper and logical format	

Developed by Michael Wagman, teacher of the gifted, School District of Springfield Township, Erdenheim, Pa.

THESIS ORAL DEFENSE RUBRIC

Name of student: _____

Thesis

1. Oral overview of position paper (5 points):
   - Did the student provide context for the thesis presented in the paper?
   - Did the student clarify the methodology of research?
   - Did the student discuss the alternate perspectives that might challenge the validity of his/her methodology or conclusions?
   - Did the student clearly state what he or she intended to prove and describe the implications if the thesis is correct?

2. Response to questions (20 points):
   - Were the answers responsive to the questions posed?
   - Did the answers demonstrate depth of understanding beyond the scope revealed in the position paper?
   - Were the answers well supported by evidence?
   - Did the student demonstrate an understanding of his/her own methodology for investigation?

3. Closing (5 points):
   - Did the student clearly summarize the most important aspects of his/her argument?
   - Did the student accurately highlight the weaknesses of other perspectives?
   - Was the student able to assert his/her thesis again with confidence and clarity?

4. Overall observations (5 points):
   - Was the student relaxed, prepared, confident?
   - Did the student use nonverbal modes of communication effectively?
   - Did the student make eye contact with his/her evaluators?
   - Did the student demonstrate clarity of thought and speech?

Oral Overview (5 points) Score/Comments	Response to Questions (20 points) Score/Comments	Closing (5 points) Score/Comments	Overall Observations (5 points) Score/Comments	Final Score and Comments

Developed by Michael Wagman, teacher of the gifted, School District of Springfield Township, Erdenheim, Pa.

RESEARCH CONFERENCE FORM

The purpose of this conference is to avoid "research holes," to ensure you have identified quality sources and haven't overlooked any significant sources or strategies before you complete your project. Schedule an appointment with the librarian to discuss your progress, and bring your sources to discuss. Be sure to schedule this appointment at least one week before your final project is due. *This conference is a project requirement. Return this form to your teacher following your conference with the librarian.*

Complete this section before your conference. Attach a working draft of your Works Consulted and/or Works Cited pages or bring along your note and source cards.

Preliminary/Working Thesis:

Subscription databases searched:

Search engines/Subject directories used:

Keywords/Subject headings searched:

Best three sources so far:

1.

2.

3.

Other valuable sources:

Problems you have encountered so far:

Complete this section during the conference

My plan for the next step:

Librarian's suggested strategies:

Student's signature _____ Class _____ Date _____

Librarian's signature _____ Date _____

CHECKLIST FOR RESEARCH

Are you doing a thorough job researching? Please complete the right-hand column. (You may ignore rows if you are certain they are not appropriate to your research.)

Attach this form to the first draft of your project. Remember to list the most promising results you find in each area.

My thesis or question _____

Did you use:			Best Result
Relevant reference books (to get a topic overview)? *Comments:*	Yes	No	
The online catalog to search for books, videos, CD-ROMs, DVDs, selected links? *Comments:*	Yes	No	
The statewide catalog, available catalogs of nearby public libraries, universities? *Comments:*	Yes	No	
Subscription services for magazine, journal, newspaper, reference materials? Which? (for instance, SIRS, EBSCOhost, bigchalk, GaleNet, FACTS.com, LexisNexis, CQ Researcher) *Comments:*	Yes	No	
A variety of subject directories, search engines, web-based databases? Which? *Comments:*	Yes	No	

Did you use:			Best Result
What were your best search terms and strategies? *Comments:*	Yes	No	
Bibliographies of the books and articles you already had to find new leads? *Comments:*	Yes	No	
Reader's Guide or other print indexes (especially for pre-1990 events)? *Comments:*	Yes	No	
Interviews? Experts, organizations, associations via email? *Comments:*	Yes	No	
Primary sources (speeches, documents, legislation, letters, songs, photographs, surveys, statistics, polls)? *Comments:*	Yes	No	
Perspective, advice, and feedback from your librarian, teacher, other adult? *Comments:*	Yes	No	

Name _____ Class _____ Date _____

Comments of Teacher/Librarian: _____

REFLECTING ON THE RESEARCH PROCESS

On a separate sheet, please reflect on the challenges and successes you found during the research process. Refer to each of the following categories, but focus on those issues that were most relevant to you as you researched.

Planning
Reflect on the process of focusing your research. What challenges did you encounter in developing a question or thesis?

Gathering
Describe any problems or successes you had as you searched. Did any particular search strategies work well or disappoint you? Which databases and search tools worked well? What were the major barriers to your search for balanced and credible resources?

Organizing
How did you ensure that your information comprehensively addressed the question, hypothesis, or thesis? How and why did you modify your original question or thesis? What strategies did you use to reorganize the information? Did these strategies lead you to connections, patterns, etc.?

Documenting
Did any issues arise as you documented your sources?

Presenting/Communicating
Were you proud of your product? Was it appropriate to the audience? How might you have improved it?

Student Name _____ Class _____

Teacher comments:

Librarian comments:

Developed in collaboration with Carol H. Rohrbach, language arts coordinator, School District of Springfield Township, Erdenheim, Pa.

COMPARING SUBSCRIPTION SERVICES AND SEARCH TOOLS (HIGH SCHOOL)

Perform the following searches (or searches relevant to your research) using the search tools listed below. In each box list the two best sources you found on the first two pages of your results list. "Best" means most relevant, reliable, credible. In choosing the best, you'll want to make sure you would be able to defend the source for inclusion on a Works Cited page for a research project.

Important: In databases, whenever possible try both the *subject* and the *keyword* search options.

| | Ask Jeeves http:// askjeeves.com/ | Yahoo! http:// yahoo.com | Google http:// google.com | SIRS Knowledge Source | | EBSCOhost/InfoTrac/bigchalk | |
				Subject	*Keyword*	*Subject*	*Keyword*
Women's rights in India							
Drug use in sports							
Hip-hop music							

Rank the five search tools from 1 to 5 (with 1 being the best) in their order of effectiveness for your research.

Ask Jeeves _____ Yahoo! _____ Google _____ SIRS _____ EBSCOhost/InfoTrac/bigchalk _____

What conclusions can you come to, based on your comparisons? When would you recommend using each search tool? How did the information you found vary with the different search tools?

COMPARING SUBSCRIPTION SERVICES AND SEARCH TOOLS (MIDDLE SCHOOL)

Perform the following searches (or searches relevant to your own research) using the six search tools listed below. In each box list the two best sources you found on the first two pages of your results list. In choosing the best, you'll want to find resources you would be able to use heavily in a research project. "Best" means most relevant to your topic and by the most reliable authors.

Important: Whenever possible, try both the *subject/browse* and the *keyword* search options.

	Ask Jeeves for Kids http:// ajkids.com	Yahooligans! http:// yahooligans.com	KidsClick! http://sunsite. berkeley.edu/ KidsClick!/	SIRS Discoverer	Searchasaurus/ Middle Search	bigchalk Library
Global warming						
Space travel						
Girls and sports						

Rank the six search tools from 1 to 6 (with 1 being the best) in their order of effectiveness for your research.

Ask Jeeves for Kids _____   Yahooligans! _____   KidsClick! _____   SIRS Discoverer _____   Searchasaurus _____   bigchalk Library _____

What conclusions can you reach based on your comparisons? When would you recommend using each search tool?

PRACTICE RANKING SOURCES (HIGH SCHOOL)

Not all sources are created equal. Imagine you are writing a paper on the problem of AIDS in sub-Saharan Africa. Your teacher has encouraged you to use a balance of primary and secondary sources. The following sources appear on your various results lists. Rank them (from 1 to 10 with 10 being the best) in terms of their relative value to your paper. Label them "primary," "secondary," or "tertiary." Consider which you could most easily defend if your teacher questioned their value. For discussion: Would your rankings change depending on the type of project you were doing?

Description of Source	Rank and Reason	Primary (P) Secondary (S) Tertiary (T)	Intended Audience
A transcript of a *20/20* interview with a physician from Doctors without Borders, found in bigchalk Library. The doctor describes the cultural reasons for the spread of the epidemic.			
An article on World AIDS Day from *People* magazine			
A current article from the *New York Times* that includes a map of the regions most heavily affected			
The article on Africa from Grolier Online offering a concise overview of the issue			
A government report on the issue from the Centers for Disease Control's website			
An article from *Science* magazine on new research developments in fighting AIDS in Rwanda.			
Congressional testimony on the global response to the AIDS epidemic by the doctor who is executive director of UNAIDS			
The website of Celebrities Fighting AIDS in Africa			
Proceedings of the 9th Conference on AIDS in Africa hosted by the University of Pennsylvania			
Newspaper analysis of a speech made by the U.S. president after a visit to a hospital in Africa			

PRACTICE RANKING SOURCES (MIDDLE SCHOOL)

Not all sources are created equal. Imagine you are writing a paper on the problem of cliques in schools. Your teacher has encouraged you to use a balance of primary and secondary sources. The following sources appear on your various results lists. Rank them in terms of their relative value to your research project. Consider which sources you could most easily defend if your teacher questioned their value. For discussion: Would your rankings change depending on the type of project you were doing? There are no right or wrong answers. The most important thing is to think seriously about the sources you use for research.

Description of Source	Rank and Reason	Primary (P) Secondary (S)	Intended Audience
"The Curse of Cliques," an article from *Time* magazine			
"Cliques I Joined," an AOL-based web page about online clubs, created by a student			
"Clique" definition, *Webster's New World Thesaurus*, third edition			
"How Peer Pressure Can Affect You," from *Current Health* magazine			
"Leaders of the Pack: Kids' Cliques Hold Sway with Power of Exclusion," from the *Boston Herald*			
Transcript of a speech by the U.S. secretary of education relating cliques to school violence			
Transcript of an ABC *Good Morning America* interview with a parenting expert and five middle-school students. The students discuss the impact of cliques on their schools.			
Email from a middle-school parent, concerned about her daughter, on the Question and Answer section of the *Parent Soup* web page			
An encyclopedia article on "cliques"			

WEB PAGE EVALUATION WORKSHEET

- This worksheet is for students to use as they analyze the sites they visit
- How much of the following information can you find on each page? Where did you find it?

	#1 Page title:	#2 Page title:	#3 Page title:
1. AUTHORITY			
What type of domain is it?	• com • org/net • edu • gov/mil/us • non-US _____ • other _____ • ~ or % or "users" or "people"	• com • org/net • edu • gov/mil/us • non-US _____ • other _____ • ~ or % or "users" or "people"	• com • org/net • edu • gov/mil/us • non-US _____ • other _____ • ~ or % or "users" or "people"
Appropriate for the content?			
Might it be a **personal page?**			
Who wrote it? Credentials? How did you find out?	• E-mail (minimum) Other evidence?	• E-mail (minimum) Other evidence?	• E-mail (minimum) Other evidence?
	Hints: Look at the URL first. In the page, scan for names and "about" links.		
2. AUTHENTICITY, SOURCES, DATES			
Authentic, not forged, not altered?	Sources well documented?	Sources well documented?	Sources well documented?
Dated? All pages the same?	Date _____ Current enough?	Date _____ Current enough?	Date _____ Current enough?
	Hints: Truncate back the URL if you cannot find a sponsor. Try checking the domain name owner.		
3. WHY? Purpose, viewpoint			
What's the page's **aim, intent?** Why was it created?	• Inform, facts, data • Explain • Persuade • Sell/entice • Share/disclose •	• Inform, facts, data • Explain • Persuade • Sell/entice • Share/disclose •	• Inform, facts, data • Explain • Persuade • Sell/entice • Share/disclose •
Who sponsors the page? Is there an "About us"?			
			Hints: Check the SIDEBAR and BOTTOM

(Continued)

Worksheet (Continued)

	#1 Page title:	#2 Page title:	#3 Page title:
Balanced perspective? Links to **other viewpoints?** Bias? Anything *glaringly* omitted?			
Possibly ironic? Satire or parody? Spoof?			
4. WHAT DO OTHERS SAY?		Hint: In Google, AltaVista, search: **link:all.or.part.of.url**	
Who links to it? Opinions of it?			
Found in any **reliable directories?**			
Comfortable citing this page in a research paper?	• Yes • No • Only if I found out	• Yes • No • Only if I found out	• Yes • No • Only if I found out

ANNOTATED WORKS CITED

Annotated Works Cited pages require you to use critical research and evaluation skills. The following guidelines apply to materials in all formats—books, magazine articles, websites, reference materials, etc.

Your most challenging task may be locating the credentials of more obscure authors. Consult *Current Biography, Contemporary Authors,* or some of our periodical and reference databases for biographical information. Search the Web for resumes.

Check with your teacher to see which of the following elements you should include in your annotations:

- Author's credentials
- Scope and purpose of the work: Is it an overview? Persuasive? Editorial?
- Comparison of the work with others dealing with the same topic or others in your Works Cited list
- Intended audience
- Brief summary of contents
- Evaluation of research: Is the work logical, clear, and carefully researched?
- Evaluation of scope: Has the topic been adequately covered?
- Evaluation of author bias
- Relative value of the work to the thesis

Example of an Evaluative Annotation

Katz, Jon. "The Rights of Kids in the Digital Age." *Wired* July 1996: 120+.

Katz, former contributing editor to *Wired* and the author of *Geeks,* presents a compelling argument for safeguarding the rights of children online. The article is aimed at a general, but computer-savvy, audience. Katz offers a far more liberal perspective than recent pieces in such major news journals as *Newsweek,* which warned the public of the dangers children face in electronic environments. Katz advocates the idea of preparing the "responsible child" and outlines the rights of such a child. He claims that our new "digital nation" requires a social contract similar to the one proposed by philosopher John Locke and adopted by the founders of our own country to protect the rights of all citizens. This comprehensive, distinctive, liberal view added needed balance to my project.

EVALUATING WEB SOURCES FOR YOUR RESEARCH PROJECT

Web Citation Author. "Title of page." *Title of larger site.* Date of publication. Name of associated institution. Date of access. <http://addressofsite.>	Authority/ Credibility Why is the author qualified to write on this topic?	Source Who is sponsoring this site? Is it a .org, .gov, .com, .edu, other?	Bias Does the site promote a particular point of view? What is it?	Relevance Does this site further my research? In what way is it relevant to my topic?	Rank Rank this site's value to you on a scale of 1 to 5 (1 is the best)

A WEBQUEST ABOUT EVALUATING WEB PAGES

If we are to maintain high expectations of students' research efforts and their information products, we need to offer them guidance and practice in the thoughtful evaluation of sources.

This WebQuest is designed to help students become better information consumers by asking them to evaluate and compare sets of web pages around a focused topic.

The full unit, teacher guide, and assessment tool are available online at http://mciu.org/~spjvweb/evalwebstu.html. The suggested sets focus on cloning, tobacco, Shakespeare, and dinosaurs, but this unit will be far more effective if a teacher selects a set of pages around a theme about to be studied and around the reading and interest levels of a particular student group.

Students work in small groups to evaluate the set of sites, ranking them from the perspective of experts in the areas of content, authority/credibility, usability/design, and bias/purpose. Each student in the group should complete his or her own organizer through the assigned perspective. A group reporter takes notes on the group's discussion and reports back during a full-class discussion in which students come to consensus regarding the relative value of the sites to research projects.

ORGANIZER FOR EVALUATING WEBSITES WEBQUEST

Evaluator's role: ____ Content ___ Authority/Credibility ___ Bias/Purpose ___ Usability/Design

Site Title	Strengths	Weaknesses	Rank
Site #1			
Site #2			
Site #3			
Site #4			
Site #5			

In one or two sentences, defend your choice for the #1 site related to the criteria you were assigned:

Organizing and Communicating

From *Information Power*

> *Standard 3:* The student who is information literate uses information accurately and creatively.
>
> *Indicators*
> 1. Organizes information for practical application
> 2. Integrates new knowledge into one's own knowledge.
> 3. Applies information in critical thinking and problem solving
> 4. Produces and communicates information and ideas in appropriate formats
>
> *Standard 6:* The student who is an independent learner is information literate and strives for excellence in information seeking and knowledge generation.
>
> *Indicators*
> 1. Assesses the quality of the process and products of personal information seeking
> 2. Devises strategies for revising, improving, and updating self-generated knowledge

From *NETS for Students*

> 3. Technology productivity tools
>   - Students use technology tools to enhance learning, increase productivity, and promote creativity.

- Students use productivity tools to collaborate in constructing technology-enhanced models, prepare publications, and produce other creative works.

4. Technology communications tools
   - Students use telecommunications to collaborate, publish, and interact with peers, experts, and other audiences.
   - Students use a variety of media and formats to communicate information and ideas effectively to multiple audiences.

5. Technology research tools
   - Students use technology to locate, evaluate, and collect information from a variety of sources.
   - Students use technology tools to process data and report results.

6. Technology problem-solving and decision-making tools
   - Students use technology resources for solving problems and making informed decisions.

From *Information Literacy Competency Standards for Higher Education* (Association of College and Research Libraries)

Standard 2: The information literate student accesses needed information effectively and efficiently.

Performance Indicators

5. The information literate student extracts, records, and manages the information and its sources.

Standard 3: The information literate student evaluates information and its sources critically and incorporates selected information into his or her knowledge base and value system.

Performance Indicators

1. The information literate student summarizes the main ideas to be extracted from the information gathered.

3. The information literate student synthesizes main ideas to construct new concepts.

4. The information literate student compares new knowledge with prior knowledge to determine the value added, contradictions, or other unique characteristics of the information.

Standard 4: The information literate student, individually or as a member of a group, uses information effectively to accomplish a specific purpose.

Performance Indicators

1. The information literate student applies new and prior information to the planning and creation of a particular product or performance.

2. The information literate student revises the development process for the product or performance.

3. The information literate student communicates the product or performance effectively to others.

RELATED POSTER

Thinking about Questions: Beyond "Topical" Research

Here's the big problem. They collect all that great information from all those fabulous sources. Then what? How do you help students transform this raw material into truly original work, work that displays high levels of synthesis and analysis, work that highlights each student's unique voice?

Students need help in the form of scaffolding, and students need guidance in developing a schema for organizing information. By explicitly "walking" them through the complicated task of transforming raw information into a finished product, with the help of checklists and organizers, we demonstrate the supporting thinking and organization skills necessary along the way. After sufficient practice and application, the skills should become internalized, the scaffolding can be removed, and the cognitive skills and habits should stand on their own.

ACTIVITIES AND HANDOUTS

Question Organizer and Sample Questions: This "brainstormer" (see p. 99) can be assigned before students begin a research project. It is designed to move students beyond topical research to the types of questions that inspire critical thought. Teachers and librarians can confer with students to help them select the most promising questions to research. Though students should use the form to brainstorm two topics related to the area they are studying, the samples here were written for two different topics to demonstrate a greater variety of question options.

Changing the Questions: Some Sample Responses: These sample responses (p. 100) will guide students toward developing their own "meatier" questions, questions worthy of their research time and energy.

Developing Essential Questions for a History Project: Students asked to develop thoughtful questions for research often need a little help. This form (see p. 101) offers a sample template to help U.S. history students think more creatively about their questions. Consider creating one for other disciplines.

Research Task Requirements Checklist: This checklist (see p. 102) analyzes the small pieces of a major project and their due dates. You may ask a class to

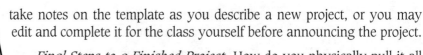

take notes on the template as you describe a new project, or you may edit and complete it for the class yourself before announcing the project.

Final Steps to a Finished Project: How do you physically pull it all together? This handout/transparency (see p. 103) lists the pieces to include for any finished product.

Thesis Project Organizer: Thesis statements drive the most commonly assigned projects, in any medium. This organizer (see p. 104), also usable for in-process assessment, will help students clarify their arguments and focus them on gathering evidence to support those arguments.

Current Events Template: Experienced one too many "so what" current events presentations? You can encourage more student thought and reflection. Use this organizer (see p. 105) with students to help them prepare to present a news item to the class. The questions are designed to move them beyond a simple summary of news, to reflect on the impact of the event and to explore their personal reactions. You might examine these organizers before presentation to evaluate students' level of preparation, or collect them for use as an assessment tool. FACTS.com uses an adapted version of this form.

Speech Organizer: This organizer (see p. 106) should help students fight their fear of speaking by ensuring they prepare compelling opening and closing statements and carefully consider the major points they need to make.

Debate Organizer: Avoid debating disasters and ensure that students walk into class feeling ready to argue. This organizer (see p. 107) may be used as a formative assessment tool to ensure students are prepared enough to participate, and as an organization tool to supplement debaters' note cards.

Persuasive Documentary Organizer: This tool (see p. 108), designed in collaboration with Theatre/Communication Arts teacher Marlene Thornton, helps students prepare video documentaries to broadcast over the school cable network. It forces students to carefully plan how they will grab the attention of their audience, focus their thesis, and dismiss conflicting opinions.

Template for Creating a Pathfinder: A pathfinder may be used as a student product in place of the formal paper. It offers students an opportunity to show off skills in searching and evaluation. Post the best projects online, as guides for future researchers. The template (see p. 109) may be pasted into students' HTML editors as a handy starting point.

Student Self-Evaluation Checklist: By asking students to sign this form (see p. 111) and attach it to their finished product, you get procrastinators to think one last time about the quality of their work, and you're likely to inspire the planners to think more carefully about the criteria you value most.

How to Score More Points with Your PowerPoints: Distribute and discuss this handout (see p. 112) before assigning a multimedia product. It will guide students toward focusing on what's truly important in delivering an effective presentation.

Storyboard for a Multimedia Presentation: Have lots of these on hand (see p. 113) as students begin to structure their multimedia productions. Consider requiring well-planned storyboards from students before they even touch a keyboard or a camera.

QUESTION ORGANIZER AND SAMPLE QUESTIONS

Changing the Questions

	Topic #1: _____	Topic #2: _____
Which one? (Collect information to make an informed choice.) E.g., Which twentieth-century president did the most to promote civil rights?		
How? (Understand problems and perspectives, weigh options, and propose solutions.) E.g., How should we solve the problem of water pollution in our neighborhood?		
What if? (Use the knowledge you have to pose a hypothesis and consider options.) E.g., What if the Declaration of Independence had abolished slavery?		
Should? (Make a moral or practical decision based on evidence.) E.g., Should we clone humans?		
Why? (Understand and explain relationships to get to the essence of a complicated issue.) E.g., Why do people abuse children?		

Brainstorm two topics related to the unit we are studying. Use the cues to develop essential questions that will help you focus your research. You don't need to fill in every box.

CHANGING THE QUESTIONS (SOME SAMPLE RESPONSES)

	Topic #1: Civil War	Topic #2: Shakespeare
Which one? (Collect information to make an informed choice.) E.g., Which twentieth-century president did the most to promote civil rights?	Which Civil War general was the best military strategist?	Which of Shakespeare's tragedies has the most relevance for today's politicians? Which of the characters in *Romeo and Juliet* is most worthy of punishment?
How? (Understand problems and perspectives, weigh options, and propose solutions.) E.g., How should we solve the problem of water pollution in our neighborhood?	How did the scientific advances of the nineteenth century affect the outcome of the Civil War? (Students might choose among advances in communications, transportation, weaponry, etc.)	How does Shakespeare's subplot help us better understand the themes of _____?
What if? (Use the knowledge you have to pose a hypothesis and consider options.) E.g., What if the Declaration of Independence had abolished slavery?	What if General Lee had had better information at Gettysburg?	What if Brutus had made the final funeral oration in *Julius Caesar?*
Should? (Make a moral or practical decision based on evidence.) E.g., Should we clone humans?	Should Confederate symbols be used in official state flags and logos today?	Should Hamlet have minded his own business?
Why? (Understand and explain relationships to get to the essence of a complicated issue.) E.g., Why do people abuse children?	Why did Great Britain favor the South during the Civil War?	Why do Shakespeare's plays continue to have meaning for today's students? Why does Shakespeare use so many references to the natural and unnatural in *Macbeth?*

Brainstorm two topics related to the unit we are studying. Use the cues to develop essential questions that will help you focus your research. You don't need to fill in every box.

DEVELOPING ESSENTIAL QUESTIONS FOR A HISTORY PROJECT

As you consider moving from a topic to a thesis for history research, consider these "starter" questions to help you develop your own thoughtful question to explore.

"How" Questions

1. How does hindsight help us understand _____?
2. How did _____ get this way?
3. How have particular lessons of the past instructed us for the future?
4. How would I have solved (how should the president have solved) _____?
5. How has _____ reflected the American dream over the course of the decades?
6. How have efforts of reform impacted _____?
7. How significant were the efforts of individuals in _____?
8. How did one area of culture influence another in a particular time period? (For instance, how did politics influence fashion? How did technology influence food?)
9. How has _____ changed over the period of _____ and why?
10. How did _____ play a role in the evolution of the _____ century (decade)?

"Which" Questions

1. Which was the best (or three best) or worst of the century/decade/era:

   Event (Lindbergh flight? lunar landing?)

   Discovery (nuclear fission? vaccines? plastics?)

   Person (artist? musician? politician?)

   Literary movement (beat period? Harlem renaissance?)

   Legal decision (*Brown* v. *Board of Education*? *Roe* v. *Wade*?)

   Amendment (Prohibition? women's right to vote? allowing eighteen-year-olds to vote? defeat of the ERA?)

2. Which were the biggest mistakes?
3. Which two decades were the most similar or most different? Why?
4. Which were the major conflicts within _____? Have these conflicts been repeated? Which resolutions, or attempted resolutions, were the most effective? How would I have advised resolving these conflicts?
5. Which period (or region) would I choose to live in? Which would I definitely not choose to live in?
6. Which were the most influential catalysts for change in this area?

"Why" Questions

1. Why did the United States _____ during this period?
2. Why did _____ (women, slaves, Native Americans, a political group, the president, foreign governments) behave or respond as they did during _____?

RESEARCH TASK REQUIREMENTS CHECKLIST

Project title _____

1. What is the due date for the completed project? _____

2. In-process steps/research package requirements. Are specific materials due during different stages of the research process?

   Preliminary or working thesis due   _____

   Pre-write/first draft due   _____

   Second draft due   _____

   Note cards/Source cards due. Required # _____   _____

   Storyboard/Outline/Organizer due   _____

   Working bibliography/Works Cited/Works Consulted due   _____

   Research conference form due   _____

3. What are the format requirements for the project? Must it be a formal paper, oral presentation, video, multimedia project? May I choose the format?

4. What is the required length in words or pages? _____

   Are there specific word-processing requirements?

5. Is a specific number of sources required? _____

6. Are specific source types required? For instance, magazine articles, newspaper articles, primary sources (speeches, letters, legislation, interviews, etc.), websites, books, scholarly journals?

   Other _____

   _____

7. Are there any source types my teacher prefers I do not use?

8. What form should my documentation take? Works Cited and/or Consulted? Annotations? In-text or in-project documentation?

9. Will my teacher require me to formally defend my research (explain my conclusions, my choice of sources, and how and why I used them)?

10. Will I have to include a reflection on the research process as part of my final product? (This might take the form of a cover sheet or journal and should describe the strategies you used, the successes and frustrations you experienced in your writing and your research, which research tools were most effective, and what you might do differently next time.)

FINAL STEPS TO A FINISHED PROJECT

The completed draft of your project should include the following:

1. A title page, containing the title, your name (and/or signature), your teacher's name, the specific class, and the date of submission

2. Acknowledgments page

3. The text/content of the project. If this is a formal paper, number only the pages of the text, beginning with page 2.

4. Works Cited

5. Works Consulted

Note: Include these sections in all projects, multimedia as well as traditional papers!

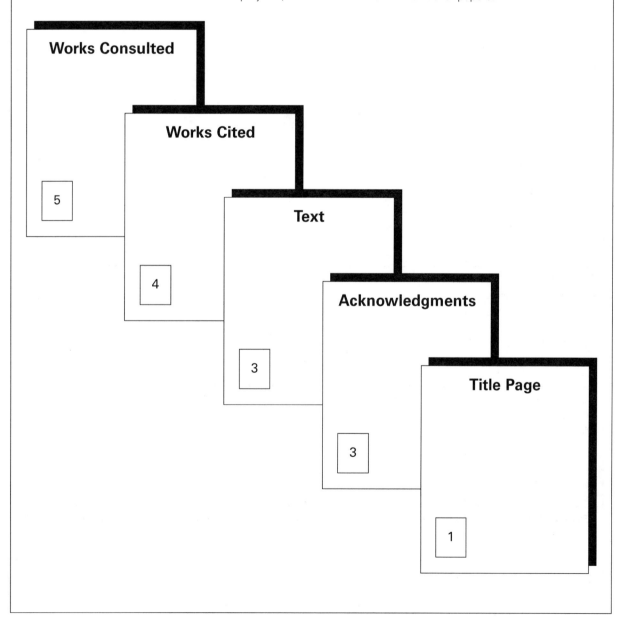

THESIS PROJECT ORGANIZER

PRELIMINARY/ WORKING THESIS:	What is the argument you plan to prove in your project? Avoid a "so what" thesis!
Supporting Argument: Evidence/Quotes:	
Supporting Argument: Evidence/Quotes:	
Supporting Argument: Evidence/Quotes:	
Examination and Refutation of Possible Opposing Arguments: Evidence/Quotes:	
Reconfirmation of Position/Thesis— Main Points	

PROJECTED CONCLUSION: Powerfully restate the stance of your thesis in light of the evidence you presented.

CURRENT EVENTS TEMPLATE

Complete the following to help you analyze the event you've selected.

ARTICLE CITATION:
WHO?
WHAT?
WHERE?
WHEN?
PRIOR KNOWLEDGE? What did you already know about this topic?
MAIN POINTS: Use keywords and "bullets," not full sentences.
AUTHOR BIAS: Supports/opposes/neutral
QUOTE: Identify a quotation to back up your assessment of the author's view or a quotation that sums up the essence of the article.
SO WHAT? Why is this news important? Who is likely to feel the impact of this news? What difference does it make?
REACTION: What is your personal reaction to this news? How does the new information change your understanding of this topic?
QUESTIONS: What issues remain unanswered? What else would you like to know?

SPEECH ORGANIZER

OPENING: Attention-getting device (story, humorous anecdote, compelling fact or statistic)	
PREVIEW: Summarize what's to come and/or make transition from opening to body of speech	
BODY OF SPEECH: Note any statistics, quotes, evidence, or visual aids that fit in with each point	**Point 1**
	Point 2
	Point 3
CONCLUSION: Deliver clincher, wrap-up, point you want to restate	
FINAL STATEMENT: What is the very last thought you want to leave with your audience?	

DEBATE ORGANIZER

RESOLVED/POSITION:

Make sure you include quotations and note sources as part of your evidence.

Argument 1:	Evidence:
Argument 2:	Evidence:
Argument 3:	Evidence:
Argument 4:	Evidence:

Anticipate! Be prepared to counter the arguments of your opposition.

OPPOSING POSITION:

REFUTING ARGUMENTS:

Argument 1:	But:
Argument 2:	But:
Argument 3:	But:
Argument 4:	But:

Clinch your argument with a strong summary, your most compelling evidence, a powerful quotation.

CLOSING:

PERSUASIVE DOCUMENTARY ORGANIZER

HOOK:

THESIS:

ESSENTIAL BACKGROUND FOR VIEWERS:

Argument 1:	Evidence/Quotes:
Argument 2:	Evidence/Quotes:
Argument 3:	Evidence/Quotes:
Argument 4:	Evidence/Quotes:

Include here the opposing arguments you plan to briefly dismiss.

OPPOSING VIEWPOINT:	RESPONSE:
1.	1.
2.	2.
3.	3.

How will you clinch your argument? What are your final words for the audience?

CONCLUSION:

TEMPLATE FOR CREATING A PATHFINDER

What is a pathfinder? A pathfinder is a guide for researchers. Pathfinders have been used in libraries for many years to save researchers time and to help them avoid frustrating dead ends. By creating a web-based pathfinder, in addition to learning about the particular resources for the topic you are exploring, you are performing a service to our library and to fellow students in our school and beyond. Creating a pathfinder will demonstrate your searching skills and your ability to discern quality information sources.

We hope to use the best pathfinders as reference tools. Do a thorough job, be creative, find the best possible resources, and publish your pathfinder appropriately and attractively. You'll definitely want to consult the librarian for advice along the way!

You may paste this template into an HTML editor to guide you as you work. Remember to create appropriate web links as you compose.

Example of an appropriate topic for a pathfinder:

> Mr. Brown's class studies the North American colonies every year. Select one of the regions he assigns (perhaps the Mid-Atlantic colonies) and prepare a tool to help researchers find maps, primary source documents, books, websites, articles in historical journals, videos, etc.

Include the following in your pathfinder. (Remember, not all categories will make sense for all topics!):

- Title, Introduction, and Scope: Introduce the topic and discuss the scope you will cover. For whom is this guide designed? Will it be focused on a particular time period? Region? How comprehensive is this tool?

- General Advice for Researchers: Are there truly important specific starting places any researcher must see before doing further research?

- Experts: Are there names that come up again and again as you search? What is their expertise? Are they scholars? Should other researchers be aware of them?

- Dewey Call Numbers/Library of Congress Numbers—Reference Works: Under which call numbers are most of the reference books in this area shelved? Annotate the most useful of these titles.

- Dewey Call Numbers/Library of Congress Numbers—Circulating Works: List these num-

bers and the subtopics with which they are associated. Annotate any titles that are critically important. If a work is truly not-to-be-missed, you might consider linking to reviews from the *New York Times,* Amazon, or other online sources.

- Print Indexes: Does the library offer any print indexes that lead to journals or other media on the topic? (Examples might be *Readers' Guide,* especially for events before 1990; *Book Review Digest; American Heritage Index*)

- Online Databases: Which subscription services would be best for this research? (For instance, specific GaleNet databases, FACTS.com, Wilson Biographies, EBSCOhost, Searchasaurus, bigchalk, SIRS, LexisNexis, CQ Researcher)

- Gateway Sites on the Internet: Are there any major guide sites (web subject directories) about your subject on the Web? If so, annotate the best so users will know why they should be visited first. You might find these gateway sites by searching directories of specialized search engines. These include: SearchIQ, LII.org (look for directories in your results), CompletePlanet, InvisibleWeb.com.

- Specific Websites: List any specific websites that may be important. Annotate the very best. If you are dealing with a controversial topic, select a balanced group of sites. If you have a good number of sites to suggest, consider arranging them into categories. Include reference and glossary-type websites. (use http://glossarist.com).

- Primary Sources: Are there key documents—letters, speeches, legislation, etc.—that are important or that lead to a better understanding of the topic?

- Image Resources: Are there particular sites that will provide researchers subject-specific images? For instance, you might recommend one of NASA's image databases for researchers in aeronautics.

- Online Journals: List any accessible, full-text journals that would be helpful to researchers. For instance, a pathfinder on "training" might link to *Runner's World Online.*

- Organizations, Associations: When appropriate, list the official sites and phone numbers of any

(Continued)

Template (Continued)

major organizations, support groups, and so on involved in the topic. If you have chosen a controversial topic, attempt balance by including representative groups on all sides of the issue.

- Video Resources: Does the library have any films or film series that will add to understanding of the topic? Or, have you discovered any videos that should be rented or purchased and viewed?

- Microfiche: Especially for history topics, microfiche offering old newspapers and magazines might be an appropriate lead.

- Additional Advice to Researchers: Here you may summarize. Remind students of strategies or offer your best advice. You may choose to address how you found your best selections—briefly note which indexes, catalogs, and search tools you used; which search strategies or terms worked best; your criteria for "quality sources"; and how to get around any issues or pitfalls other researchers might face. In the advice area, you might also suggest keywords/phrases/subject headings and related terms that would work best for researchers. Consider synonyms, names of noted experts, organizations, etc. When appropriate, demonstrate use of searching syntax—for instance, include phrases in quotation marks. Did you discover any surprising subject headings as you browsed through database results?

- Additional Categories: What else is important to know for the topic of study? For instance, for a topic relating to travel, you might add such categories as currency converters, airfare, hotel directories, or translating services.

- Sign and Date your pathfinder.

Model pathfinders can be found at these sites:

- Internet Public Library http://ipl.org/ref/QUE/PF/
- Camden County Library System's Pathfinders and Reference Guides http://www.camden.lib.nj.us/web/pathguide.htm
- Homework Center at Multnomah County Library (web-based resources only) http://www.multnomah.lib.or.us/lib/homework/index.html
- Pathfinder for Constructing Pathfinders (samples and guidance) http://home.wsd.wednet.edu/pathfinders/path.htm
- Pioneer Middle School Pathfinders http://pio.wsd.wednet.edu/library/path.htm

An online version of this template is available at http://mciu.org/~spjvweb/pathfinder.htm/.

STUDENT SELF-EVALUATION CHECKLIST

Name _____ Date _____

Teacher _____ Course _____

Please attach this sheet to your finished project.

1. Clearly state the hypothesis, question, or problem your research attempts to address or answer.

2. Write a three-to-five-sentence abstract summarizing your research.

3. I have fulfilled all the requirements listed on the assignment sheet.	☐ Yes	☐ No
4. My thesis or question is adequately answered.	☐ Yes	☐ No
5. My evidence is logically organized.	☐ Yes	☐ No
6. I have carefully checked spelling, grammar, and punctuation.	☐ Yes	☐ No
7. My verb tense is consistent throughout.	☐ Yes	☐ No
8. I have varied sentence structure to make the text more readable.	☐ Yes	☐ No
9. My paragraphs have topic sentences.	☐ Yes	☐ No
10. Transitional sentences link my paragraphs.	☐ Yes	☐ No
11. I have effectively and responsibly quoted, paraphrased, and summarized.	☐ Yes	☐ No
12. My introduction and conclusion clearly support my question/thesis.	☐ Yes	☐ No
13. My documentation is correctly formatted.	☐ Yes	☐ No
14. All facts not commonly known are documented.	☐ Yes	☐ No
15. I have used a balanced and adequate number of relevant resources.	☐ Yes	☐ No
16. My project is neatly published and appealing to the reader.	☐ Yes	☐ No
17. I have chosen an effective method of presentation.	☐ Yes	☐ No
18. My own voice, as a writer, is clearly heard.	☐ Yes	☐ No

19. I have not plagiarized any of the material in this project.

Signature _____

Please list your comments about the research process on the back of this form.
What would you do differently next time?

HOW TO SCORE MORE POINTS WITH YOUR POWERPOINTS

The point is . . .

Here are some tips for improving your multimedia presentations.

Content counts big time!

- Begin by preparing a storyboard or use the program's outlining tool to help make sure your project is logically structured and effectively delivers your message.

- Focus on your content. Make sure your presentation shows evidence of solid research and your own high-level thought.

- Know your message. What is the essential question? Or, what is your thesis? Your audience does not need to know "everything you know about X."

- Spelling errors look even worse when projected! Proofread like crazy.

- Respect copyright by citing every piece of borrowed text as well as every piece of media you use, other than copyright-free clip art. Unless items are cited throughout, the last slide should list your Works Consulted, no matter how informal the presentation. Use only small portions of media elements. The *Fair Use Guidelines for Educational Multimedia,* at http://www.libraries. psu.edu/mtss/fairuse/guidelinedoc.html, set limits for the amount of borrowed material acceptable for use in student and teacher products.

PowerPoint is more powerful in the hands of a powerful *presenter.*

- Practice! Rehearse even if it feels silly. Use family, friends, and pets as well as your mirror.

- Engage your audience by making frequent eye contact and displaying enthusiasm.

- Tell stories. Personal anecdotes and clever examples are far more compelling than bullets, no matter how they fly in.

- Grab your audience by starting with a clincher— a powerful quotation, a story, an anecdote, a statistic, or a surprising fact.

- Speak clearly and slowly. Avoid using slang and filler words.

- Look good. Dress appropriately.

- Be flexible. Do not read straight from your notes and slides.

- Keep it simple. Leave words out; summarize rather than cram. Limit the number of points per slide, so the audience does not struggle, reading to keep up. Unless you are quoting, full paragraphs have no place in your presentation.

- End with the exact point you want your audience to remember.

- Convey your own excitement for your presentation. Consider every presentation as a valuable present, a gift for your audience. What you give them should change them in some way. It's about you. There are no magic bullets.

Design matters.

- All graphic elements are messages. Your medium should match your message. Choose a consistent look that enhances rather than detracts from your theme. All slides and transitions should look as if they are part of the same presentation. Understand both your message and the audience and adjust your text and art accordingly. A presentation on the Holocaust would not be effective with a cute font and silly cartoons.

- Use sounds and animations cautiously. They can distract from your message. Reserve multimedia for emphasizing important points.

- All bullets should be readable from the back of the room. Combinations of uppercase and lowercase letters are the most readable.

- Create and use original art. Your own drawings and digital photographs pack far more punch than tired clip art. Why spend hours searching for the perfect image of a flower when you could far more effectively draw one or shoot one with a digital camera? If you must use clip art, consider combining it with other elements—for instance, incorporating clever thought bubbles.

Consult your teacher's rubric to make sure you understand exactly what he or she expects.

STORYBOARD FOR A MULTIMEDIA PRESENTATION

Name _____ Page #_____

Slide/Card	Slide/Card Image and/or Description	Story/Text/Source
#_____		
#_____		
#_____		

Joyce Kasman Valenza is the librarian at Springfield Township High School Library (Erdenheim, Pa.) and the techlife@school columnist for the *Philadelphia Inquirer.* Valenza is the author of *Power Tools* (ALA, 1998) and the video *Internet Searching Skills* (Schlessinger), a YALSA Top Ten Award winner. She has taught courses in searching skills for Chestnut Hill College and Mansfield University. Valenza speaks nationally on issues relating to libraries, education, and information-literacy skills and contributes regularly to *Classroom Connect, Voice of Youth Advocates,* and other educational journals. Her school web page (http://mciu.org/~spjvweb) won the IASL School Library Web Page of the Year Award for 2001. Her personal web page is http://neverendingsearch.com.